Revolutions
in Knowledge

Revolutions in Knowledge

Feminism in the Social Sciences

EDITED BY
Sue Rosenberg Zalk
and Janice Gordon-Kelter

Westview Press
BOULDER • SAN FRANCISCO • OXFORD

Copyright © 1992 by Westview Press, Inc.

Published in 1992 in the United States of America by Westview Press, Inc., 5500 Central Avenue, Boulder, Colorado 80301-2847, and in the United Kingdom by Westview Press, 36 Lonsdale Road, Summertown, Oxford OX2 7EW

Library of Congress Cataloging-in-Publication Data
Revolutions in knowledge : feminism in the social sciences / edited by
  Sue Rosenberg Zalk and Janice Gordon-Kelter.
    p. cm.
  Includes bibliographical references.
  ISBN 0-8133-0584-5
  1. Feminist theory. 2. Feminism—Research. 3. Social sciences—
Methodology. 4. Women social scientists. I. Zalk, Sue Rosenberg.
II. Gordon-Kelter, Janice.
HQ1190.R49 1992
305.42—dc20   91-27461
                                                                    CIP

Printed and bound in the United States of America

 The paper used in this publication meets the requirements
of the American National Standard for Permanence of Paper
for Printed Library Materials Z39.48-1984.

10   9   8   7   6   5   4   3   2   1

The editors dedicate this book to Joan Kelly (1926–1982),
feminist historian, for her activism on behalf
of women's studies at the Graduate School, CUNY,
and to the feminists in the CUNY system for the
community and unwavering resolve to provide
CUNY students with a more balanced education

CONTENTS

PREFACE AND ACKNOWLEDGMENTS

This book evolved from a lecture series sponsored by the Center for the Study of Women and Society at the Graduate School of the City University of New York in 1987 and 1988. Rebecca Blank, Cheryl Townsend Gilkes, Virginia Held, Dorothy Helly, Mary Brown Parlee, and Joan Tronto presented earlier versions of their chapters at the seminar. These have been updated and expanded. Susan Farrell was kind enough to contribute an introduction on feminism and sociology to serve as a context for Gilkes's case study. Jane Roland Martin presented her chapter as the inaugural lecture for the Project on the Study of Gender and Education, Kent State University and University of Akron, November 18, 1988. One of the editors (SRZ) had the good fortune to hear it and to secure permission to include it in the book. We are extremely grateful to all of the contributors for their commitment to the project.

We would also like to thank the staff of the Center for the Study of Women and Society: Lakshmi Bandlamudi, Patricia Belcon, Rosaria Caporrimo, Seung-kyung Kim, Margaret Logreira, Maria Rivera, and Gale Smith. Appreciation is extended to the individual social science programs and to the Feminist Students' Organization at the Graduate School for their support of the seminars. Finally, we would like to express our gratitude to our editor, Spencer Carr of Westview Press. It would be difficult to find a better person with which to work.

Sue Rosenberg Zalk
Janice Gordon-Kelter

1
FEMINISM, REVOLUTION, AND KNOWLEDGE

Sue Rosenberg Zalk
and Janice Gordon-Kelter

This book is not simply a review and analysis of the contributions feminist scholars have made to the study of women and to the social sciences. Though all the authors provide a perceptive overview of the history and status of feminist scholarship in their disciplines, the essays provide a foundation for developing critical themes for the future: Is feminist scholarship transforming the social sciences at the most fundamental levels? Will this scholarship result in a reconceptualization of the practice of social science? What directions should feminist scholarship take?

The contributors to the book analyze the assumptions of their disciplines, hold these up against the research and scholarship feminists are producing, and assess how well the study of women "fits" or does not fit into the standard paradigms of their disciplines. They comment on the challenges presented and the evolving revisions and offer views on the transformations of their disciplines that will be needed if they are to produce what can be thought of as adequate knowledge.

The book begins with a chapter on philosophy, a discipline traditionally categorized as one of the humanities and not a social science. This is done with a clear purpose. Philosophy, as an intellectual discipline, has been influencing the social sciences for over two thousand years, and, indeed, all social sciences can trace their roots to philosophy, having emerged as independent disciplines as recently as the late nineteenth and twentieth centuries. It is instructive to note how often the points Virginia Held makes in her survey of philosophy reemerge in the chapters that follow.

We have called this book *Revolutions in Knowledge: Feminism in the Social Sciences*. Some, undoubtedly, will scoff at the very idea of a feminist revolution, especially one in knowledge. As the chapters ahead reveal, the contributors to this book differ considerably in their analyses of the nature of the changes in their disciplines as a result of feminist work. Although they all acknowledge change and trace its historical roots, offer examples of feminist perspectives, and suggest what is missing and what must yet be done, there is no consensus as to whether these changes constitute a revolution. The debate would expand with an even greater diversity of opinions were the sample of feminist scholars widened. Nevertheless, we stand by our title.

Revolution, as we use the term, refers not to a final outcome but to a continuing process. We believe that feminism constitutes a revolutionary challenge to the academic disciplines here examined. Although feminism's opponents may reject this challenge, they must do so by attending to it. Mainstream scholarship must address feminist issues, not only because the number of revolutionaries is growing but also because their critiques are maturing and can no longer be ignored. Whether the revolution maintains or increases its momentum remains to be seen, but we believe a revolution in the social sciences is in process.

The Revolutionary Nature of Feminism

Feminism is both an intellectual-moral perspective and a socio-political movement. In both forms it has, ultimately, revolutionary goals. As an intellectual and moral vision, it challenges, among other things, basic social structures and the foundations on which they rest. As an organized social and political effort, it systematically embraces particular issues and gathers resources with which to target various aspects of gender oppression, with the aim of overcoming the hierarchy of gender.

Feminists' political and social strategies, especially at a global level, may appear to have limited reformist aims. They seek to revise certain laws and change certain attitudes. They operate within existing systems and concentrate on the chipping away of certain parts of these systems that contain and sustain gender inequities, such as governmental regulations, corporate policies, or medical practices.

Feminism, in this form, adopts a gradualist strategy. This gradualist strategy has witnessed many successes, but it has drawbacks. It is laborious and slow and, as is evident in recent political shifts and legal rulings in the United States, hard-fought-for gains can, with considerably less effort on the part of the opponents, be taken away.[1] In a political atmosphere marked by backlash, substantial energy and resources may have to be directed toward defending and maintaining even the modest gains that have previously been achieved. Change is not a steady, linear progression. The gradualist strategy is to assure that the progression continues.

This strategy of gradualism, however, is only part of the reality of the feminist movement. A focus on feminism as a moral-intellectual movement indicates that the social changes feminists seek involve aspects of culture and thought that are absolutely central to the social, political, and economic organization of societies. Existing social systems have evolved from assumptions that are built into their very design, and assumptions about gender are among the most fundamental. Consequently, what appear to be limited challenges to social institutions on grounds of gender inequity often constitute fundamental challenges because they are built on a deeply different conceptual basis. Social systems are not only inherently unreceptive to feminist revisions but also basically unable to accommodate such revisions without the kind of redefinition and reorganization that would indeed count as revolutionary.

Intellectually and morally, feminists envision societies in which gender stratification has been overcome. Practically, this vision means that the feminist movement specifically targets for change those aspects of society that promote and sustain the oppression of women—gender inequities and gender stratifications. But the feminist vision is more global. Feminists seek not just a world in which women are equal participants and contributors, but one that is founded on feminist principles. We do not know what that world would look like, for it has never existed, and of course there is disagreement and debate about the principles themselves. Speculative visions, though, are often found in fictional and philosophical writings.[2]

What are these feminist principles? Allowing for disagreements and for differences in emphasis, we can say that on the whole feminists tend to advocate societies that are not characterized by relations of domination and subordination for anyone, societies where all people are free and equal and live with respect and dignity, where power and resources are not hoarded by an elite few who define social values and dictate institutional processes to all others. Feminists often value the humane principles traditionally characterized as "female," principles that have been trivialized and devalued. Feminists advocate institutions that promote such values as nurturing, caring, mutual concern, and cooperation and champion societies in which opportunities and roles are not a function of gender or race or class.[3]

Societies founded on these principles would require major social transformations of existing societies, and few would posit that the gains of the women's movement suggest the realization of this vision within the foreseeable future. Thus, does our claim that feminism constitutes a revolutionary movement have only theoretical validity and lack practical implications? We think not.

We think such a claim has practical value because of the essential role the organization of gender plays in any society. Every success promoting greater gender equality diminishes the gender power hierarchy that operates within and supports all systems and institutions be they political, economic, familial, religious, or intellectual. The diminution of gender stratification entails the redistribution of power and resources, and while one cannot guarantee that this shift will lead to the realization of a feminist vision, one can expect that it will lead to a different society. When one grasps how threatening the prospect of eliminating gender stratification is to those who benefit from it, then both its pivotal place in the social structure and the revolutionary potential of feminism and the women's movement become apparent.

Feminism, then, challenges standard societal arrangements, the assumptions and values from which they have evolved and from which they continue to be defended, and the existence of institutionalized systems that support and reproduce them. But what does a feminist revolution have to do with *knowledge*, with what we know?

The Feminist Challenge to Knowledge

A revolution in knowledge implies a radical change in the way we obtain and interpret knowledge as well as a rethinking of much of what we think we know. The possibility of such a revolution in the social sciences is not readily embraced either by mainstream social scientists or by the public. But, as we shall see, when women are brought adequately into the purview of the social sciences, the composition of what the social sciences take as knowledge can change dramatically.

The new feminist challenges to knowledge reflect the larger feminist movement. They exist within the same context and struggle with many of the same oppositions. They also confront similar basic questions. Can the foundations on which the social sciences evolved accommodate feminist perspectives on knowledge without fundamental change, without a revolution in knowledge? How different is the picture of these disciplines when viewed through a feminist perspective? The authors of the chapters that follow answer these questions.

Methodologies and the Social Sciences: The Scientific Model

Social scientists do not ask us to accept on faith the information they provide. They are researchers, pursuing knowledge in accordance with the standard and systematic methodologies of their disciplines. These research procedures, modeled after those of the physical sciences, are designed to elicit objective, value-free findings, to minimize (if not completely eliminate) the possibility of bias and subjectivity—to render findings as unrelated as possible to the perspective and situation of the researcher.[4] The value of these methodologies appeared obvious. As Dorothy Helly notes in her discussion of the historical profession, "Scientific historians . . . viewed the aim of the profession as objectivity. Because their methods were 'scientific,' their results must represent implicit truth" (Chapter 9).

This search for truth through objective methodologies characterizes all of the social sciences, whether they employ the empirical experimental procedures of the psychologist, the historian's recreation of the past through the study of primary sources, or the employment of mathematical formulas to explain economic behavior. "Good" research renders the researcher irrelevant to the data, nothing more than the conduit for revealing reality. The "purest" way to assure this objectivity is to rely on numbers, and measurement is frequently the favorite design. The subject of study is reduced to what can be objectively measured, and what can be objectively measured can be assigned a number that represents quantitative or qualitative significance. Once assigned numbers, data can be analyzed statistically. The attractiveness of this approach lies in the claim to scientific objectivity, for, as we all know, "numbers do not lie."

Social scientists acknowledge that bad research exists, and all disciplines have among their ranks poor researchers, people who employ inappropriate methods or use them carelessly or whose personal biases enter into the execution of the research and obviously affect the data. But as the social scientist would point out, this is a technical problem— the fault lies with particular individuals, not with the methodological approach of the discipline as it is conceptualized. Each discipline monitors itself to avoid the misrepresentation of research data. Studies are scrutinized; researchers must answer to their colleagues; findings must be replicated. Social scientists do not claim to have perfected their methods. They recognize that they could and should be more exact, and each discipline has among its ranks those who dedicate themselves to improving and expanding the tools of the profession.

While all of these limitations should caution the prudent not to accept at face value the revelations of any one study, they do not constitute a meaningful challenge to the credibility of the social sciences nor discredit the basic foundations of the field. The scientific paradigms, the theoretical models, the research tools, all remain intact. The discipline is not called upon to question them, merely to improve upon them.

Rebecca Blank takes this perspective on the role of feminism in economics when she states that "the standard economic model of individual behavior has not been so strongly challenged" and that gender-related debates occur among those who "agree on certain fundamental assumptions about individual economic behavior" (Chapter 7). Economics, with its emphasis that rational beings make interest-maximizing choices, tends to be unconcerned with the broader implications of human behavior. Thus, economic models accept that discrimination against women occurs and focus on such topics as discrimination's effects on wage differentials or employers' choices.

Although Blank stresses the conservative nature of the economics profession and downplays the role that feminism has so far played in reshaping the discipline, she and others still note that within the standard economic paradigm changes do occur. New research topics have emerged in economics that focus on gender differences, and the new approaches of feminist economic thinkers do broaden the limits of the paradigm itself. Further, challenges to the paradigm emerged out of the work of those in other disciplines and, Blank notes, criticism of the "economic paradigm out of an explicitly feminist perspective" is beginning to be voiced by a small group of economists.[5]

In seeing feminism as having a limited effect on the fundamental assumptions in her field, Blank is the minority voice in this book. While the other authors differ in the degree to which they believe a revolution in knowledge is in progress, they agree that a feminist perspective within their disciplines can cause significant alterations in the fundamental methods and approaches of the fields and, thus, in what their fields offer as knowledge.

Feminism in the Academy

Feminist skepticism about the ability of the social sciences, as they are presently constructed and practiced, to adequately address women's experiences specifically and the diversity of human experiences in general emerges naturally from a linked and overlapping sequence of scholarly challenges. This skepticism represents a qualitative leap in intellectual inquiry and is the product of a maturing feminist movement within academic institutions.

Women's studies/feminist studies evolved as part of the women's liberation movement of the late 1960s—but *this development was and is a scholarly-academic movement.* Nonetheless, the women's movement was central to the evolution of this new intellectual wave. The politics of the times supported the collective efforts of feminist scholars (usually women) to voice discontent with their disciplines' treatment of women. Women organized within their disciplines, and their organizations reduced feelings of isolation and alienation and provided a political base and structure from which to fight these inequities. The original impetus was a response to gender discrimination within their professions. But women were not only marginalized as social scientists, they were also marginalized as subjects of inquiry. Women, it soon became apparent, were invisible in the bank of knowledge that constituted the social sciences.

Many scholars recognized that much remained to be learned about women's lives. Feminist scholars in all academic disciplines began the search for knowledge about women. Historians searched the records for notable women, psychologists studied gender differences, political scientists investigated the politics of the family, and anthropologists challenged "Man the Hunter" with "Woman the Gatherer." The proliferation of this new scholarship on women continues to be impressive, as is the growing number of scholars who pursue the study of women as their specialization or who are at least cognizant of its relevance to their work.

Scattered topical courses on women sprang up in social science and humanities programs in the late 1960s and by the late 1980s were no longer unusual. Women's studies, as a distinct academic program, first appeared in the United States in 1970. Publishers, recognizing a profitable market, compete for manuscripts on women's issues and frequently promote them under the category "women's studies." Disciplinary journals, the primary vehicle for informing professionals about the most recent research and writing in their fields and the best indicator of the "mood" of the profession (e.g., topics and methodologies judged appropriate and important), regularly include articles on the study of women. Journals specifically founded as forums for feminist scholarship and gender research have established their credibility in academic circles.[6]

These developments constitute a pivotal era in the history of higher education. Women's studies programs and courses remain the most effective route for assuring the inclusion of scholarship on women in the curriculum and for giving students the opportunity to be exposed to knowledge and perspectives not otherwise easily available. Women's studies programs and courses are an essential foundation for the advancement of feminist scholarship. Nonetheless, they do not, and cannot, constitute a balanced curriculum.

Relegating feminist scholarship to programs and topical courses about women suggests that women are an atypical subgroup—a special interest topic—but not integral to the substance of the discipline. (The study of people of color has received the same treatment.) If we have research and courses on people in general and special topics courses on women (or people of color) in particular, the implication is that these latter deviate from our basic paradigm of people. If the social sciences continue to pursue and teach general principles of human behavior, but the majority of the world's population requires special attention (e.g., topical courses, specialized areas of study), which people constitute the sample from which the knowledge and standards are based? This ghettoization of feminist studies, both within the academic disciplines and the larger education institution, has functioned to promote tolerance of its existence while maintaining traditional disciplinary approaches, assumptions, and biases.

Meaningful knowledge and education must reflect the diversity of human experiences and perspectives. Efforts to "mainstream" content on women (and people of color) into basic academic courses continue with accelerating momentum. But the ghettoization of this material remains a pattern—women are treated as a subunit—a topic covered within a course or a section so labeled in a textbook. Correcting this bias is a major challenge. The legacy of disciplinary perspectives is enduring, increasingly engraved into the academic foundation with the passage of time.[7]

Curricula reflect the research and scholarly activities of professionals in the disciplines, and the efforts of feminist scholars are fueled by the growing interest in obtaining knowledge about women's experiences. Increasing numbers of researchers and scholars in the social sciences and arts and humanities are using the tools of their disciplines to gain and expand knowledge about women.

Is it enough for our revolution in knowledge that scholars apply the traditional methods and theories of their disciplines to investigate women as subjects of inquiry and that this material claims an increasingly larger portion of the knowledge base? We, and most of the contributors to this book, would answer "No."

A Different Perspective

Although recognizing the importance of these necessary first steps, we argue that simply adding women as a variable (or people of color or people of poverty) will never result in a body of knowledge that reflects the diversity of human experience. The best that could be achieved is "equal time," rather than an unbiased account of human behavior. A truly balanced curriculum or discipline could not evolve from this tactic because the disciplines were not designed to study women and are unable to do so in ways that allow for meaningful insights. Indeed, if this assessment is accurate, we can speculate that the continuing treatment of the topic of women as a subunit within the disciplines may reflect not only academicians' resistance to feminist scholarship but also the mismatch between the study of women and existing disciplinary boundaries.[8]

The social sciences paid homage to the ideal of objectivity, but as women as a topic of inquiry received increasing attention it became clear that men's experiences and actions are not universal and what is uncovered about men cannot serve as a standard for research on women. The supposedly objective social sciences presented a view of reality that offered dominant groups the picture it pleased them to see (Held, Chapter 2). Rather than being politically or morally neutral, mainstream methods and language were more "likely to reproduce or at least leave unchallenged the ideological discourses that justify and recreate the social relations of gender" (Parlee, Chapter 3). Further, the suggestion was made that the social sciences' emphasis on "value-free" objectivity would, by definition, exclude a feminist perspective. As Joan Tronto states, "any type of scholarship that began from a clear political perspective would be suspect" (Chapter 6).

Not only scholarly goals but also methods of research, inquiry, and teaching were called into question. Noting the competitive, cutthroat atmospheres within which scholarly exchange and learning were supposed to occur, feminists asked, "Is competition truly superior to cooperation? Is this how inquiry ought to proceed?" (Held, Chapter 2). In the classroom, the adoption of a "gender-sensitive ideal as opposed to either an illusory gender-free one or a vicious gender-bound one" seemed to offer women a better way of learning (Martin, Chapter 9).

The rigid division between public life (male, subject to historical change, appropriate for scholarly consideration) and private life (female, eternal, outside disciplinary boundaries) was also called into question. Historians found historical change in the study of the family or of sexuality; political scientists found power relations within families as revealing as those within governments. Anthropologists and sociologists learned to go "where the action isn't" (Rapp, Chapter 5).

As the line between public and private blurred, so did artificial distinctions between self and society. The male tendency to perceive objects and beings as discrete and autonomous was supplemented, or even supplanted, by a female emphasis on dependence and connectedness. (See discussions on the work of Carol Gilligan in Chapter 3 by Parlee and Chapter 2 by Held.) Parlee describes psychological approaches that begin, not with an individual psyche, but with human activities, allowing for a focus that includes "both the individual and her or his culturally defined environment as a dynamic, mutually constituting system" (Chapter 3). Sociologist Cheryl Townsend Gilkes finds analysis of black women's experience meaningless without the connection to community. For her, "it is black women's relationship with their entire community . . . that facilitates a unique intersection of race-ethnicity and class as a motive force for social change" (Chapter 4).

A Turning Point in Knowledge

The social sciences were developed for the most part by a homogeneous group of educated white, middle-class, Western men who pursued their search for knowledge by building on shared assumptions and observations. But assumptions shape observations, and observations are understood in terms of assumptions. From this closed circuit, theories were articulated and evidence for their validity sought.

As the pages ahead reveal, the academic disciplines evolved from the study of men—men's experiences, perspectives, values, needs, social roles, judgments, and interests. They grew out of men, with the assumptions of men, studying men. They reflect the world through the eyes of a select, atypical group existing within a larger society. The exclusion of women from the development of the disciplines has resulted in the male as the model of human behavior. The study of the female, if structured on that model, can do little more than suggest women's atypical status. The very potential for revealing the complexity of human behavior and experiences are limited, and as such, inaccurate by the very terms and limitations of the models.

Trained in the tradition of social science inquiry, feminists typically began their work using the discipline's tools to study women's roles in society and topics specifically pertinent to women. This approach gradually led to the discovery that the assumptions, theories, constructs, and methodologies that define a social science's perspective are inadequate for studying and explaining women's experiences as experienced by women. Theories are supposed to reflect experiences, not the other way around. If they do not explain most people's lives, theories are not valid, and the social sciences that rest on this structure have a suspect knowledge base. We judge this revelation as the turning point for a feminist revolution in knowledge in the social sciences.

Within the past two decades, at a rate and abundance unparalleled in the history of the social sciences, feminist scholars have contributed research and scholarship in the forefront of their fields. We know of no movement in the social sciences that can boast as rich, rapid, and revisionary a body of scholarship as can women's/feminist studies. And we know of none more challenging to the practice of social science or more suggestive of transformations in knowledge.

Is such a revolution necessary? Audre Lorde has argued that "the Master's tools will never dismantle the Master's house."[9] As the pages that follow reveal, the majority voice in this book calls for the building of a new, more inclusive structure. Is such a revolution in knowledge in process now? Knowledge is passed from generation to generation. This is an inherently conservative process, and breaking through with new paradigms takes time. In many ways this dismantling and rebuilding requires a new beginning, but it is this reconceptualization of the disciplines that holds the promise of a true revolution in knowledge.

Notes

1. In the United States, the most obvious recent example of the rapidity with which major advances in women's rights can be reversed is the series of state legislative actions restricting women's access to legal abortions. These laws followed the July 1989 Supreme Court ruling in *Webster* v. *State of Missouri*, which granted states greater authority to determine the legal status of abortion. Although this ruling did not *officially* reverse the *Roe* v. *Wade* (1973) Supreme Court decision that abortion was the personal right of a woman (in consultation with her physician), in application it has resulted in the passage in some states of legislation that renders legal abortion services virtually inaccessible to most women. Similar patterns of retreat from actions to correct gender inequities can be found in legislators' attempts to reinterpret affirmative action laws as they apply to government funding and taxes.

2. A bibliography on these visions would be most lengthy. Ruby Rohrlich and Elaine Baruch's, eds., *Women in Search of Utopia: Mavericks and Mythmakers* (New York: Schocken Books, 1984) is a cross-cultural anthology depicting Utopias of the past, contemporary utopian experiments, and Utopia fiction and science fiction. Carol Pearson's review of feminist Utopias is most informative ("Women's Fantasies and Feminist Utopias," *Frontiers* 2, 1977, 50–61). See also Sara Ann Ketchum's article "Female Culture, Womanculture and Conceptual Change: Toward a Philosophy of Women's Studies," *Social Theory and Practice*, 6, 1980, 151–162. There are many excellent novels depicting feminist communities. *Sultana's Dream*, written by Rokeya Sakhawat Hossain and first published in 1905 (New York: Feminist Press, reprinted 1988), is most impressive for its simple presentation of complex issues and for the author's creation of technologies unknown at that time and taken for granted today. It is highly recommended. Feminist science

fiction writers have provided creative visions of ideal societies. Some suggested readings are *The Female Man* by Joanna Russ (New York: Bantam, 1975); Marge Piercy's *Woman on the Edge of Time* (New York: Knopf, 1976); and Ursula LeGuin's *The Left Hand of Darkness* (New York: Harper and Row, 1976). Charlotte Perkins Gilman's *Herland* (New York: Pantheon, 1971, first published in 1915) is a classic and should not be overlooked.

3. Although there is no universally agreed-upon party line on feminist principles and feminist debate on this theme is ongoing, the principles put forth here are basic and not very controversial. Several of the authors in this book discuss feminist principles and their relationship to the social sciences. Held, Tronto, and Martin pay particular attention to this theme in their chapters and have publications that explore the topic in greater depth. The reader is referred to their chapters for further information and resources. *Feminist Frameworks*, edited by Alison M. Jaggar and Paula Rothenbery Struhl (New York: McGraw-Hill, 1984), is an excellent overview of the variety of views among feminists on issues of concern to women.

4. Three excellent works that explore the myth that the methods of "scientific" inquiry have led to value-free, unbiased research are: Sandra Harding and Jean F. O'Barr, eds., *Sex and Scientific Inquiry* (Chicago: University of Chicago Press, 1987); Ruth Hubbard, Mary Sue Henifen, and Barbara Fried, eds., *Women Looking at Biology Looking at Women: A Collection of Feminist Critiques* (Cambridge, Mass.: Schenkman, 1979); and Evelyn Fox Keller, *Reflections on Gender and Science* (New Haven: Yale University Press, 1985).

5. Of all the social sciences, economics, with a standard paradigm for individual economic behavior and a basic reliance on mathematical logic and formulas for predicting and explaining economic decisionmaking, comes closest to adhering to the methodological model of the physical sciences. Thus, like the physical sciences, scholars' claims that the basic assumptions of their disciplines do not have any inherent gender bias supports rapid rejection of challenges to that assumption. Blank's analysis reflects the present status of feminist influence on the discipline of economics and the dominant view of the parameters within which a feminist perspective will affect economic theory and research. While many feminist economists are not part of mainstream economist circles, there are economists who believe that a feminist perspective could ultimately alter the discipline. Because their writings tend to be nontraditional, these scholars frequently publish in nonmainstream journals, journals in other fields (e.g., sociology journals), or journals specifically founded to provide them a forum (e.g., *Review of Radical Political Economics*). Robert Cherry, in his book *Discrimination: Its Economic Impact on Blacks, Women, and Jews* (Lexington, Mass.: D. C. Heath and Company, 1989), expanded the traditional economic arena of perspectives and questions, and benefits from the research and insights provided by scholars in other social science disciplines. This book is most informative and written for noneconomists. Although they do not represent a powerful presence in the discipline, feminist critiques of the standard economic model of individual decisionmaking are increasingly appearing in print. See, for example, William Darity, ed., *Labor Economics: Modern Views* (Boston: Kluwer-Nijhoff,

1984); Julianne Malveaux, "Comparable Work and Its Impact on Black Women," *Review of Black Political Economy*, 1985.

6. See, for example, *SIGNS, Sex Roles: A Journal of Research, Gender and Society, Psychology of Women Quarterly, Frontiers, Women and Politics, Women and History, Women's Studies International Quarterly, SAGE: A Scholarly Journal on Black Women.*

7. Although we are concerned here with scholarly challenges to standard social science paradigms, assumptions, and derived knowledge, we should not underestimate the essential role women's organizing and activism (both within their disciplines and the larger academy) has in the existence and credibility of these challenges. The feminist movement within the social sciences has enabled feminist scholars to question the basic assumptions of their disciplines, pursue original research that extends beyond traditional disciplinary boundaries, and publicly challenge their colleagues, who are more in number, more powerful, and more secure in their cushion of the discipline's history. The impressive impact Carol Gilligan's research has had in both the social sciences and arts and humanities is an excellent example of this point. The chapters authored by Held and Parlee discuss the content and theoretical and methodological contribution of Gilligan's research. The point we would like to stress, though, is her research's place in the politics of the times. In short, Gilligan's research on moral development threw doubts on assumptions of universal, linear stages of cognitive development. It exposed blatant gender biases in a substantial and credible body of research, biases that treat values as facts and place them in a hierarchy of development that devalues women. As a result, Gilligan challenged some of the most powerful and respected professionals in her field (psychology). What is more, this research was first undertaken as a doctoral dissertation. Although the absolute number of scholars appears large, the professional community within any one discipline is tight and mavericks are easily pushed aside. Most graduate students know that the politics of the discipline and their academic program cannot be ignored in their efforts to obtain a Ph.D. This instance was not the first time individual voices were raised in protest against accepted doctrines on women. From its inception there were dissenters in the field of psychology. Challenging the establishment is dangerous. The risks are great— censorship and discrediting, failure to be tenured or promoted, denial of funds to pursue research. How do Gilligan and others like her dare take on the "establishment," the men in power and their following, and get away with it? Only with organized activism of professional women's groups within the disciplines and the support, visibility, credibility, and power they provide are the voices of feminist scholars heard and not silenced.

8. It should be noted that the interdisciplinary community of women's studies scholars was an important factor in this realization. Women's studies programs were not simply a tactical approach to establish a vehicle for educating students about women and gender biases in the canon. It became readily apparent to women's studies scholars that the interests and methodologies of a single discipline could not accurately reflect the complexity of people's lives. Women's studies programs asserted their academic legitimacy as an area of study that

crossed over traditional disciplinary biases and constraints. The growing number and increased presence of women's studies communities encouraged faculty to become knowledgeable about feminist scholarship in multiple disciplines. From this movement emerged expanded perspectives, which have had an impact on the theories and research feminists bring to their disciplinary work. As is evident in positions put forth by many of the contributors in this book, this interdisciplinary perspective is an important component in the transformations they judge necessary for their disciplines to provide meaningful knowledge.

9. Audre Lorde, *Sister Outsider* (Trumansburg, N.Y.: Crossing Press, 1984), 112.

2
CHANGING PERSPECTIVES
IN PHILOSOPHY

Virginia Held

It is now widely recognized, thanks to feminist agitation, that scholars in most traditional disciplines have overlooked to a remarkable degree the history, writings, thought, and contributions of women. Recent feminist scholarship, however, is now going far beyond filling in the gaps resulting from such oversight. Feminist scholarship often calls for radical revisions in the way in which inquiry should proceed in philosophy, the social sciences, and even the natural sciences. It suggests that perhaps what we have taken to be real or scientifically valid may be based on male rather than on fully human experience, and it suggests that what were thought to be the leading candidates among acceptable normative and empirical theories may need to be drastically changed if the experience of women is to be accorded as much importance as the experience of men.

The first phase of feminist scholarship focused on a tremendous one-sidedness among the fields of inquiry. Women were simply not in the picture. History, for instance, was the history of men and not of women. The social sciences studied those topics that concerned men or studied them from the point of view of men. Feminist scholars called attention to these gaps and biases. Attention was then paid to filling in some of the large empty spaces that were apparent and to correcting certain obvious biases. Topics such as employment patterns among women, housework, rape, women's health, marriage, and family violence became legitimate objects for scholarly study. More attention was paid to the work of women in literature and the history of thought.

In the course of bringing women into the picture, it also became possible to see that if women were brought into the picture, the picture would have to be very different. It was not just a matter of adding material here and there, of filling in omitted material; gradually we began to see that the whole picture might have to be redrawn, rethought, reconceptualized. For instance, if as much attention is paid to women as to men, the great periods into which history has been divided might have to be changed. When Joan Kelly asked the question, "Did women have a Renaissance?" the answer turned out to be: No. Maybe the high points for men were the low points for women, and history from the point of view of women might look entirely different.[1]

As we looked ahead and considered how the fundamental principles of freedom and equality on which democracy is supposedly founded should be applied to women, it began to be recognized how fundamental the changes would have to be: Not only did the extent to which such principles had not been applied to women in the past become apparent, but it also became clear that if women were to be brought fully into the public domain of government and work, private life would have to be very different. The notions of what was public and what was private and why economics and political science and anthropology and sociology construed them the way they did were brought into question. And the relative importance and value of these domains were sometimes turned upside down.

New Assumptions

Feminist scholars are now suggesting that the changes in what we think of as knowledge and how we should go about trying to acquire it may have to be very deep indeed. Just as paying attention to class has caused us to see many things very differently, paying attention to gender causes us to rethink much of what we thought we knew. Some people go even further, suggesting that the changes feminist inquiry will bring will be even more fundamental than those brought about by Copernicus or Darwin or Freud. This is not a far-out view expressed by someone at the radical fringes, but the view of Carolyn Heilbrun in *Academe*, certainly a mainstream journal.[2]

Discovering Reality by Harding and Hintikka[3] is one of the best collections that suggests where some of this inquiry is going and how, at the most fundamental level, basic assumptions are going to have to be revised if we are to avoid taking male experience as the equivalent of human experience. It is a collection of philosophical essays about epistemological issues in many fields. I will try to present a few highlights from this volume in order to indicate the kinds of suggestions that are being made. Of course, for these new ways of thinking to prevail against ways that are for all of us deeply entrenched, a lot of hard argument will be required. Few of us are competent to offer sustained argument in fields far from our own. My own inquiries are in social and political philosophy and ethics, and I shall try to argue for some new ways of thinking in these areas. But I include some points from other fields to suggest that the skeptical doubts being raised by feminists about standard conceptions have certain aspects in common from one field to another.

Philosophers, dealing as they do with metaphysical and epistemological issues, raise questions that are relevant to all fields of inquiry. Let us begin with an example. Everything that we say has to begin with certain ontological assumptions about what is real. All inquiry requires such assumptions. It would really be startling if we found that our ways of thinking about reality itself were male ways rather than universal ways. Yet this possibility needs to be considered. The Harding and Hintikka volume includes a paper by the philosophers Merrill Hintikka and Jaakko Hintikka that suggests just this.[4] The usual metaphysical assumptions made by the sciences are that there are entities that have properties. Yet studies seem to show that boys tend to bracket together objects or pictures of objects whose intrinsic characteristics are similar, whereas girls attach more weight to the social and relational characteristics of the entities to be considered. In short, women are generally more sensitive to and more likely to assign more importance to relational characteristics—that is, interdependencies—than are men and are less likely to think in terms of independent, discrete units. Conversely, males generally prefer what is separable and manipulatable. The Hintikkas pointed out that if we put a premium on the former feature, we are likely to end up with one kind of cross-identification and one kind of ontology. If we follow the guidance of the latter considerations, we end up with a different ontology. It is very astonishing to suppose that one's fundamental assumptions about reality may be gendered assumptions; of course, all this is still speculative. But it would be most interesting to have the kind of psychological and philosophical research that would enable us to evaluate whether and how we ought to revise our assumptions about reality; such issues seem eminently worth exploring.

In a lucid and readable short book, Genevieve Lloyd showed that the very concept of reason so central to the history of human thought has been constructed from a male point of view.[5] Although the forms and details have differed from one period to another, the notion of what reason is and what it should do has been developed in terms of a repudiation of what has been taken to be characteristic of women. Rationality, Lloyd showed, has been conceptualized as transcendence of the feminine.

Consider Descartes's conception. He himself suggested that his method would open up the way for knowledge to be accessible to all and that even women might understand something of what he wrote. The more lasting influence of his philosophical views, however, was to increase the polarization of previously existing contrasts, so that mind and body came to be seen as completely distinct. This polarization, Lloyd suggested, provided a basis for the sexual division of mental labor that has persisted since that time. Women's task came to be seen as preserving the sphere of the intermingling of mind and body to which the man of reason repairs for solace, warmth, and relaxation. And women came to be associated not only with a lesser presence of reason but also with a different kind of intellectual character from which "man" has to disassociate himself in order to be "the man of reason."

Gender Concepts

Books such as these make clear why feminist inquiry should be of interest to everyone. The extent to which our past concepts, theories, and frameworks may have been gender biased and may have represented the male rather than the universal point of view makes feminist scholarship essential to the development of more adequate human understanding. If the very concepts of reality or of being rational or of achieving selfhood require that women deny their femininity, of course women cannot be fitted into the philosophical and other traditions from which they have been excluded. Nor, of course, should they want to be fitted into these traditions.

Increasingly there is the suggestion, among those pursuing these matters, that what have been taken as universal may not be male experience or male concepts but rather the experiences and conceptions of males in a given time and place, roughly Western Europe and the United States in relatively recent centuries. We do not know whether these tendencies are likely to remain partly fixed or whether they may change a great deal under different circumstances. But suggestions about the differences, at least in our own society, in the way females and males construe things are being made concerning many fields, and many of these related skeptical doubts about the adequacy of standard views take a similar form in different fields.

Consider psychology. Routinely, psychologists think about the objects of psychology in terms of individual human entities with particular psychological states, such as emotions, beliefs, and so on. To think this way—that particular psychological states attach to us singly—is not the only way we could conceptualize the material of psychology; this position should at least be defended rather than merely assumed. Skeptical doubts about whether this position is the right way to see what psychology ought to be about have been raised by the philosopher Naomi Scheman in the Harding and Hintikka volume.[6] She believes that this way of looking at things represents the way in which males in a society such as ours, where the ideology of liberal individualism is entrenched, are apt to construe the objects of psychology. However, it is undercut by female experience, if female experience is seen in its own terms rather than as a kind of defective male experience.

Scheman wrote that "this largely unquestioned assumption, that the objects of psychology—emotions, beliefs, intentions, virtues and vices—attach to us singly (no matter how socially we may acquire them) is, I want to argue, a piece of ideology. It is not a natural fact, and the ways in which it permeates our social institutions, our lives, and our sense of ourselves are not unalterable."[7] She argued that "the individualist assumption" underlies contemporary philosophical accounts of the nature of the objects of psychology, however these accounts differ from each other. The assumption is substantive, not merely formal, and the underlying reasons that might be advanced for it are inadequate. The experience of women suggests that relations between persons are as fundamental as individuals and their states.

Turning to another area of inquiry, that of evolution, there are suggestions that perhaps the kinds of interpretation that are more characteristic of male ways of looking at things have been imposed on the data collected rather than being the only or the most plausible interpretations. In another paper in the Harding and Hintikka volume, the authors suggested that evolution is the story of progress, of improvement, of expansion. "Its episodes and events express the familiar sorts of processes and characteristics which men think promote progress and create history: competition, struggle, domination, hierarchy, even cooperation—but only as a competitive strategy."[8] These are the aspects of the story that have so far been noticed. A number of other kinds of processes and characteristics do not appear in the familiar accounts of evolution. Among them are nurturance, tolerance, intention, and awareness, benignity, collectivism. These aspects can certainly be found if they are what is looked for. Altruism does in fact agitate debates in evolutionary biology, but mainly because scientists struggle to explain it away by reducing it to unintentional cooperation resulting from instinct or the competitive advantage of expectation of future reciprocation. Competition is seen everywhere even when the observed behavior is an effort to avoid it. In the view of critics, seeing competition avoidance as a motive underlying noncompetitive behavior "simply projects it even where it manifestly is not."[9] In their view, there could well be other ways of telling the evolutionary story.

Questions of these kinds are being raised and perhaps they can be disposed of with further inquiry or perhaps they will lead to quite significant reformulations or revisions in some of the most basic assumptions being made in many fields. I cannot myself argue seriously for these positions in psychology or biology or even metaphysics, but I can report that they are positions being supported. I myself argue for comparable suggestions in the areas of ethics and social and political theory.

Before doing so, let me emphasize an important consideration about whose point of view should be given the benefit of the doubt in many of these matters: the established point of view or the point of view, in this case the feminist one, that challenges established views. Nancy Hartsock put the argument very well: She argued that it is in the interest of established groups to conceal the ways in which they dominate others and benefit from keeping other groups subordinate.[10] Consequently, we can expect that the interpretation of reality they present will be distorted in characteristic ways. We can notice, for instance, that the suffering of dominated groups is often ignored, redescribed as enjoyment, claimed to be justified as freely chosen or as deserved or inevitable. The members of dominant groups, because of the ways they are insulated, are often deluded by their own ideology. Because they experience the existing organization of society as on the whole satisfactory, they interpret reality in ways that tend to support that system. Subordinate groups, however, experience the system as unsatisfactory, and their suffering motivates them to discover what is wrong with the established views of reality and of how society ought to be organized. They thus have an interest in developing new and less distorted ways of understanding the world. Women in contemporary society experience a distinct form of subordination, and their position allows them to have a distinctive epistemological standpoint. From this standpoint, Hartsock suggested, it is possible to have a less biased and more comprehensive view of reality than bourgeois science has offered or than its male-dominated, left-wing critics have provided.

The Conduct of Inquiry

Let me turn briefly to a quite different kind of suggestion, a suggestion about how inquiry ought to proceed in a more practical and embodied sense rather than in a theoretical sense. This has to do with what we might think of as the style of inquiry. I will use philosophy as an example because I am familiar with it, but much of what I say is applicable to other fields.

A leading philosophy department recently invited a well-known philosopher to give a series of lectures. Other philosophers were brought in to comment, and, as is characteristic in such arrangements, the main speaker was offered as a target against which others would launch their attacks. The philosophers brought in to attack the main speaker were referred to by the chairman of the department, and in certain cases by the commentators themselves, as the "heavy guns." One of them was introduced as "the Clint Eastwood of Midwestern philosophy." It is a picture one comes across frequently in philosophical debates and in other academic discussions. Inquiry is presented as a contest between gladiators, as a spectacle put on for graduate students and junior faculty members. If scientific research is conducted in a laboratory by a team, this enterprise may well be described with considerable envy as an "empire." It will have a section "chief," a "divisional director" or perhaps a "czar" with his surrounding courtiers. The research team will be hierarchically organized with the strong in charge.

Some women can learn to play these games of inquiry in these ways and to do so well. They hardly ever get to be the heavy guns or the big chiefs, but a few at least get tenure and can pursue work that interests them. However, feminists are increasingly asking: Is this the way the game ought to be played? Is this how inquiry ought to proceed? When feminist scholars get together for meetings, the atmosphere is often noticeably different. It is a more cooperative search for understanding with much less combativeness and possessiveness. Women working together are more apt to organize the work in nonhierarchical ways and to see it less as a competitive contest. Perhaps this is a better way to conduct inquiry, although it may have to be done outside the "strongest" departments.

Moral Development

Let me turn now to the domain of moral theory and the realm of social and political philosophy. An area in which a lot has been said about the differences between men and women is the area of moral development. The psychologist Lawrence Kohlberg at Harvard studied the moral development of children and concluded that in their development, children go through various stages during which they approach moral problems in certain characteristic ways.[11] From an early stage of worrying about whether they are likely to get caught and punished, they progress to a final stage not reached by everyone in which they decide what to do on the basis of universal moral principles, and they decide how to act out of respect for these principles. When further studies were made using these stages as a basis of interpretation, some showed that girls do not progress as well as boys.

Carol Gilligan, who had worked with Kohlberg, became suspicious of the claim that girls are less morally advanced than boys.[12] She pointed out that Kohlberg's studies leading to his interpretation of moral development in terms of "stages" and to his conclusions about what to count as "progress" were based entirely on studies of boys. Kohlberg, following Piaget, had merely assumed the development of children could be understood by considering boys only. Gilligan found when studying girls and women that they seemed to approach moral problems differently. Girls and women seemed to speak in what she called "a different voice." The question of whether it is a defective voice or just a different voice or even perhaps a better voice is an open question.

Kohlberg's final stage has a remarkable resemblance to Kantian morality. Disagreements among philosophers illustrate that not only girls seem to have doubts as to what is really the best way to approach moral problems. One philosopher had her students rank the great philosophers of the past on the Kohlberg scale; hardly any got to Kohlberg's highest stage. Possibly Kohlberg is correct in depicting this stage as the highest stage of the approach he is studying. But in the view of Gilligan and various feminist moral philosophers, when one listens to the moral reasoning of women, one can discern ways of interpreting moral problems and of organizing possible responses to them that are different from any of the established moral approaches, including Kohlberg's. Women seem to be more concerned with context than are those who take the approach Kohlberg admired, and they seem to rely less on abstract rules.

Some psychologists dispute the claim that men and women score differently on Kohlberg's scale, showing that when education and occupation are similar, so are the scores.[13] But such findings miss the point, which is that the scale itself may have been constructed from a male point of view and that women who score equally with men may just have been socialized to think like men. Gilligan is now thinking in terms of two main perspectives in the interpretation of moral problems: She and others call them "the justice perspective" and "the care perspective." The justice perspective—the Kantian one—emphasizes moral principles and individual conscience. The care perspective, in contrast, pays more attention to people's needs and to the relations between actual people; it considers how these relations can be kept in good condition or repaired if they are damaged.[14]

A number of feminist philosophers are trying to construct the kind of moral theory that would be compatible with the experience of women.[15] The experience of women does differ from that of men in ways that may be significant, whether or not Gilligan's version of how to describe this difference can succeed in being empirically confirmed to a degree that will overwhelm skeptics. Gilligan uses the duck/rabbit figure (a figure which may appear either as a duck or a rabbit depending on one's perspective) as a metaphor, suggesting that the care perspective and the justice perspective are alternative ways of interpreting moral problems. The point of this figure, in Gilligan's view, is that one can interpret moral problems from the justice perspective or from the care perspective, but not from both at the same time. When the other perspective is pointed out, one can see it, but the two ways are alternatives and they organize what is seen differently. Both men and women can recognize both moral perspectives, but Gilligan's research indicates that men have a strong tendency to employ a justice approach while a substantial proportion of women but not of men employ the approach of care.

One of the problems studied by Kohlberg concerned whether a man named Heinz should steal a drug. He could not afford to buy the drugs his ill wife desperately needed and the druggist would not lower the price. What should Heinz do? The boys Kohlberg studied organized the problem in terms of principles concerning the relative importance of life versus property. At the upper stages of development they concluded that Heinz ought to steal the drug because life has precedence over property. Girls responding to the problem were less willing to see it as a one-shot dilemma that could be solved by logical ordering. One of them, Amy, worried that if Heinz stole the drug and went to jail his wife would have no one. Amy thought maybe Heinz could borrow the money or appeal further to the druggist, and she argued that people should share so that such problems would not arise. On Kohlberg's scale she showed indecisiveness and an unwillingness to challenge authority. In Gilligan's interpretation she was expressing an ethic of care. Her world, Gilligan wrote, is a world of relationships and psychological truths in which a recognition of the relationships between people gives rise to a recognition of responsibility for one another.

Gilligan's further studies support her empirical claims, but the issues are often less empirical than conceptual. Conclusions are often matters of interpretation. To an outsider, it certainly looks as if a great deal of psychology is a matter of interpretation, and one should not ask for less interpretation when constructing feminist theory than one is willing to put up with when considering nonfeminist theory. Gilligan's work has struck a remarkably responsive chord among women, many of whom see their own experience as confirmation of her positions. At least they are convinced that there are issues here that ought to be pursued.

Childrearing

One important question that arises is, What could causally explain the differences, if they do exist, between how men and women approach moral problems? Are these differences brought about by historical circumstances or are they due to something less subject to historical modification?

Many feminists have seen Nancy Chodorow's theory of childhood development as a possible explanation.[16] Chodorow's theory concerns the different effects on boys and on girls of having women as the primary caretakers of children. If we look at such theories, we can be led to some strong recommendations for changes in childrearing practices. The activity of mothering engaged in only or primarily by women is probably bad for children and bad for society. It may create boys deprived of the ability to empathize with others and to deal with relationships, and it may create girls who have too much trouble thinking of themselves as separate individuals. Perhaps in a nonsexist society with dual parenting, the differences now apparent between men and women in perceptions of reality or in approaches to morality would largely disappear. Obviously we cannot yet know, but we can explore such suggestions.

Gilligan believes, for instance, that the explanation for the differences she finds may be that the early capacity of boys to adopt the care perspective is pushed aside by stereotypes of masculinity. We just do not know the force of social expectations, but we can be sure that they are considerable. A story about a couple trying to raise a child with nonsexist expectations illustrates the influence of social expectations. It is a true story, reported in an academic journal.[17] An academic couple wanted to bring up their children, a boy and a girl, to ignore rules about sex roles and to think that as long as the behavior was acceptable for either a boy or a girl, it was acceptable. It was all right, for example, for a boy to play with dolls and for a girl to wrestle. Realizing that the children did need a definition for gender identity, they provided it in terms of anatomy and taught their children that boys have penises and girls vaginas, but that this distinction does not indicate how they ought to behave. One day when their son Jeremy was four years old, he decided that he would like to wear barrettes in his hair to nursery school. Another little boy ridiculed him and told him over and over in the course of the day that only girls wear barrettes. Finally Jeremy got fed up and pulled down his pants to show the other boy that he was a boy even if he was wearing barrettes. The other little boy was not impressed and said, "Everybody has a penis; only girls wear barrettes." The strength of sexual stereotypes is obviously very great.

Moral Theory

A number of feminist philosophers are trying to explore what an ethic of care might look like if it were worked out as a moral theory.[18] These inquiries are still exploratory, but I will give a brief indication of where they may be headed.

One important development is that much more attention will be paid than in the past to the domain of particular others. Traditionally, ethics has paid attention to the individual self or ego, on the one hand, and to the universal "everyone" or "all rational beings," on the other. Ethics has traditionally dealt with these poles, trying to reconcile their conflicting claims. This approach has called for universalization or impartiality against the partiality of the egoistic self, or it has defended the claims of egoism against such demands for a universal perspective. In seeing the problems of ethics as problems of reconciling the interests of the self with what would be best for everyone, moral theory has neglected the wide intermediate region of family relationships, of friendship, and of relations where one feels concern for particular others. Contemporary moral philosophy has paid little attention to the morally significant phenomena of sympathy, compassion, human concern, and friendship.[19] Standard moral philosophy has construed personal relationships as aspects of the self-interested feelings of individuals, or it has let close others stand in for the universal other. Neither of these approaches is satisfactory. They especially neglect the experience of women.

The region of particular others is a distinct domain where what becomes artificial and problematic are the very "self" and "all others" of standard moral theory. In the domain of particular others, the self is already closely entwined in relations with others, and the self is at least in part constituted by the relations it is in. The relation between mother and child may be more real, salient, and important than the interests of either self in isolation. But the "others" in this picture are not the "all others" or "everyone" of traditional moral theory or of what a universal point of view could provide. They are particular flesh and blood other persons for whom we have actual bodily feelings. Moral theories will have to pay far more attention than they have in the past to this neglected realm of particular others if the theories are to be adequate. In doing so, problems of egoism versus the universal point of view look very different and may recede to a region of background insolubility and relative unimportance.

The important problems may then be seen as how to guide or maintain or reshape the relations, both close and distant, which we have or might have with actual human beings. Particular others may be actual starving children of Africa or the actual expected children of future generations and not just those we are close to in any traditional context of family, neighbor, or friend. But particular others are not "all human beings" or "the greatest number" of traditional moral philosophy.

What reasons are there to think that moral theory might be different if we adopted the point of view of the experience of women? Sara Ruddick has discussed some of the considerations that arise in the context of mothering.[20] The practice of mothering calls for maternal thinking that is, in her view, different from the thinking that arises from other contexts. Maternal practice, she said, responds to the historical reality of a biological child in a particular social world. The moral thinking that arises in such practice differs from traditional moral thinking. Ruddick sees humility and cheerfulness as values that emerge from the practice of mothering. (These traits should not be confused with self-effacement or cheery denial, their degenerative forms.) If such valuings emerge from mothering and on reflection are endorsed as moral values appropriate to this practice, we can assert that the morality of persons who mother, and not just the activities and attitudes of such persons, is different from those of persons who do not mother, because the values of this morality are the values of a distinct practice.

If we acknowledge that a mothering context is an appropriate one in which to explore moral values, an acknowledgment only prejudice could lead us to deny, then paying attention to this context, as feminist moral philosophy does, can lead to different moral theories than ignoring it. Even if the moral theories that would result from paying attention to the context of mothering would resemble those familiar from other contexts, the theories would be different in the sense that they had been tested in a context that had previously been ignored. If the relationship between mother and child should be taken as the paradigm social relationship, rather than as just another peripheral one, a possibility I will briefly consider later, then a moral theory that could be suitable to a mothering context would have a claim to priority over other candidates for moral theory.

In the views of rationality that emerged from Greek thought and were developed in the Western philosophical tradition, reason was associated with the public domain from which women were largely excluded. If the development of adequate moral theory would be best based upon experience in the public domain, the experience of women so far would be less relevant for such a development than the experience of men, because opportunities for women to participate in public life have been so limited. But that the public domain is the appropriate locus for the development of moral theory is among the tacit assumptions of existing moral theory being effectively challenged by feminist scholars.

The context of caring for particular others may be as fully appropriate a context from which to devise adequate moral theory as the context of the *polis*.

The reliability of the experience of engaging in the process of moral inquiry should be presumed to be as valid in the case of women as in the case of men. Taking a given moral theory such as a Kantian one, and deciding that those who fail to develop toward it are deficient, is imposing a theory on experience rather than letting experience determine the fate of theory, moral or other. If one holds that experience should determine the fate of moral theory, certainly one is talking about a very different view of experience than the standard empirical view.[21] But as long as women and men experience different problems and as long as differences in approaches to moral problems are apparent, moral theory ought to reflect the experiences of both. In the world of moral theory, men ought not to have a privileged position in which their experience counts for more. If anything their privileged position should make their experience more suspect rather than more worthy of being counted.

Social Theory

Finally, let me suggest a few possible implications of feminist speculations concerning what society is and should be. When we bring women's experience fully into the domain of moral consciousness, we may be able to see how limited rather than how general are contractual relations between rationally self-interested persons.[22] Instead of being central or fundamental to society or morality, as such contractual relations are often pictured as being, they may appear to be special relations appropriate only to quite particular regions of human activity. The more central and fundamental social relation seems to be that of mother or mothering person and child. It is this relation that creates society and recreates it. It is mothering persons who turn biological entities into human social entities. It is mothering persons who produce children and create language and symbolic representation and human culture for the next generation. It is thus mothering persons who, through their activities, produce and create human society. Mothering, then, is among the most human of human activities.

Despite the implausibility of it when one stops to think about it, the assumption is often made that human mothering is like the mothering of other animals rather than being distinctively human. In accordance with the traditional distinction between the family and the *polis*, and the assumption that what occurs in the public sphere of the *polis* is distinctively human, it is assumed that what human mothers do within the family belongs to the sphere of the "natural" rather than to the distinctively human. Or, if it is recognized that the activities of human mothers do not resemble those of the mothers of other animals, it is claimed that the difference is far narrower than the difference between what humans do and what animals do when humans take part in government, in industry, or in producing art. But the reality seems very different. Human mothering is completely different from the mothering of animals for whom language and morality are not available. The human mother or mothering person constructs with and for the child the human social reality of the child. The child's understanding of language and of symbols and of norms occurs in interactions between child and caretaker. Nothing seems more distinctively human than this. In comparison, government can be thought of as similar to the governing of ant colonies, industrial production as similar to the building of beaver dams, exchange as the relation of a large fish that protects and a small fish that breeds. The conquest by force of arms that characterizes so much of human history can be compared to the aggression of packs of animals. But the imparting of language and culture, the creation within and for each individual of a human social reality, and the expression of these in the stories and games of mother and children seem utterly human.

We should recognize that society arises in the relationship between mothering persons and children, rather than supposing that society arises from a contract between Robinson Crusoe–like individuals coming into existence by themselves in a state of nature. In comparison with the social bond between mothering person and child, the transactions of the marketplace seem peripheral and the laws they uphold beside the point. The relationship of exchange between buyer and seller has often been taken to be the model of all human interactions. The social contract tradition has seen this relation as fundamental to law and political theory as well as to economic activity, and rational choice theory and some contemporary moral philosophers see the contractual relation as the relation on which even morality itself should be based. The marketplace relation has become so firmly entrenched in both our empirical and normative theories that it is rarely questioned as a proper foundation for description and for normative recommendations extending far beyond the marketplace. An enormous amount of thinking then is built on the concept of rational economic man. Relations between human beings are seen as arising when they serve the interests of rational contractors. In the society imagined, based on assumptions about rational economic man, connections between people become no more than instrumental. But such instrumental connections are entirely unsatisfactory as the basis on which either to construct society or to understand it.

If, conversely, the relation between mothering person and child in an envisioned nonpatriarchal society is taken as paradigmatic for social relations, the competition and desire for domination characteristic of rational economic man may be seen as a very particular and limited human connection acceptable, if at all, only to a highly restricted marketplace. Such a relation of conflict and competition can be seen as unacceptable for establishing the social trust on which public institutions ought to rest[23] or for upholding the bonds on which caring and regard must be based. Instead of seeing the relation between mothering person and child as peripheral and anomalous, and rational exchange as central, we might reverse the location of the heart or foundation or core of society. Relations between mothering persons and the future shapers of social reality might seem central, while the transient exchanges of rational calculators might seem relatively peripheral. An acceptable society might be one that was guided, first of all, by what would be good for its children.

The Visibility of Gender

I will conclude with the question that is the title of Sandra Harding's own paper in the Harding and Hintikka volume: "Why has the sex gender system become visible only now?" Harding considers how such a fundamental variable organizing almost all of human life in every culture could have been so invisible for so long. It is an excellent question. Of course much work recognizing the importance of gender was done before the current wave of feminist inquiry. Still, gender domination was relatively invisible to most scholars and citizens until quite recently. Another question we should never lose sight of is: How did gender domination become so obscured? Each time, even after the curtain had begun to be drawn from it, it became hidden. How could this happen? How did men succeed, over and over in history, in covering up what had begun to be revealed of the gender domination that existed, shrouding it once more in obscurity after all those early glimpses? It is amazing how philosophy, supposedly the most rational and impartial of inquiries, can have been so oblivious for so long to the realities of gender domination, and it is also amazing how the supposedly objective, value-neutral, and disinterested social sciences could have managed so efficiently not to see the oppression of women for so long. It is amazing how the rest of society, and other academic fields, could have accepted the views of reality presented by the social sciences that offered the dominant groups in society the views of reality it pleased them to see.

We should not forget this as we pursue the new perspectives of feminist inquiry.

Notes

1. Joan Kelly, "Did Women Have a Renaissance?" in *Becoming Visible: Women in European History*, ed. Renate Bridenthal and Claudia Koonz (New York: Houghton Mifflin, 1977).

2. Carolyn G. Heilbrun, "Feminist Criticism in Departments of Literature," *Academe* 69(1983):5.

3. Sandra Harding and Merrill B. Hintikka, eds., *Discovering Reality: Feminist Perspectives on Epistemology, Metaphysics, Methodology and Philosophy of Science* (Dordrecht, Holland: Reidel, 1983).

4. Merrill B. Hintikka and Jaakko Hintikka, "How Can Language Be Sexist?" in *Discovering Reality*, ed. Harding and Hintikka.

5. Genevieve Lloyd, *The Man of Reason: "Male" and "Female" in Western Philosophy* (Minneapolis: University of Minnesota Press, 1984).

6. Naomi Scheman, "Individualism and the Objects of Psychology," in *Discovering Reality*, ed. Harding and Hintikka.

7. Ibid., p. 226.

8. Michael Gross and Mary Beth Averill, "Evolution and Patriarchal Myths of Scarcity and Competition," in *Discovering Reality*, ed. Harding and Hintikka, p. 72.

9. Ibid., p. 78.

10. Nancy C.M. Hartsock, "The Feminist Standpoint: Developing the Ground for a Specifically Feminist Historical Materialism," in *Discovering Reality*, ed. Harding and Hintikka.

11. See especially Lawrence Kohlberg, *The Philosophy of Moral Development* (San Francisco: Harper and Row, 1981) and L. Kohlberg and R. Kramer, "Continuities and Discontinuities in Child and Adult Moral Development," *Human Development* 12(1969):93–120.

12. See Carol Gilligan, *In a Different Voice: Psychological Theory and Women's Development* (Cambridge: Harvard University Press, 1982).

13. See especially Lawrence J. Walker, "Sex Differences in the Development of Moral Reasoning: A Critical Review," *Child Development* 55(1984):677–691.

14. See especially Carol Gilligan, "Moral Orientation and Moral Development," in *Women and Moral Theory*, ed. Eva Feder Kittay and Diana T. Meyers (Totowa, N.J.: Rowman and Littlefield, 1987).

15. See Virginia Held, "Feminism and Moral Theory," in *Women and Moral Theory*, ed. Kittay and Meyers and papers by Kathryn Pyne Addelson, Seyla Benhabib, and Marilyn Friedman in that volume. See also Annette C. Baier, "What do Women Want in a Moral Theory?" *Noûs* 9:1(1985):53–63.

16. Nancy Chodorow, *The Reproduction of Mothering* (Berkeley: University of California Press, 1978).

17. Sandra Lipsitz Bem, "Gender Schema Theory and Its Implications for Child Development: Raising Gender-aschematic Children in a Gender-schematic Society," *Signs: Journal of Women in Culture and Society* 8(1983):598–616.

18. See note 15 above. See also Nel Noddings, *Caring: A Feminist Approach to Ethics and Moral Education* (Berkeley: University of California Press, 1984).

19. See Lawrence A. Blum, *Friendship, Altruism and Morality* (London: Routledge and Kegan Paul, 1980).

20. Sara Ruddick, "Maternal Thinking," in *Mothering: Essays in Feminist Theory*, ed. Joyce Trebilcot (Totowa, N.J.: Rowman and Allenheld, 1983).

21. See Virginia Held, *Rights and Goods: Justifying Social Action* (New York: Free Press/Macmillan, 1984; Chicago: University of Chicago Press, 1989), especially Chapter 15.

22. For further discussion, see Virginia Held, "Non-contractual Society: A Feminist View," in *Science, Morality and Feminist Theory, Canadian Journal of Philosophy* Supplementary Volume 12(1987):111–137.

23. See Virginia Held, *Rights and Goods*, especially Chapter 5. See also Annette Baier, "Trust and Antitrust," *Ethics* 96(1986):231–260.

3
FEMINISM
AND PSYCHOLOGY

Mary Brown Parlee

Feminist psychological research has developed through stages similar to feminist scholarship in other disciplines. First there was recognition and documentation of the neglect of women and women's experiences— or, more accurately, documentation of the fact that the experiences and actions of some men had been misleadingly presented as universal. Then came recognition that the concepts and theories developed to provide an understanding of men's experiences are often inadequate for understanding women. This revelation led to the effort to identify and study neglected problems of particular interest to women or problems defined in the popular/political discourse as "women's issues."[1]

During the dozen or so years covered by these three phases of feminists' interactions with traditional psychology (from the late 1960s to the early 1980s), feminist psychologists built an organizational base within the field. Feminist women and some supportive men increasingly gained access to positions of power in professional organizations, positions affecting a wide range of activities important in determining what the knowledge base in psychology is or can be. (These include editorships of major journals, memberships on powerful boards and committees, key staff positions, and major elective offices.) From some points of view, the impact of such activities by feminists has dramatically changed the way psychology functions as an organized discipline.

- Research articles submitted for review to journals published by the American Psychological Association (APA) are now reviewed "blind" (with the author's name and institutional affiliation removed)
- These journals have officially adopted a policy of nonsexist language use,[2] and it is reasonably well monitored and enforced

- Guidelines for avoiding sexism in research have been published[3]
- Substantial program time at national and regional conventions is in effect earmarked for feminist research about women, and as a consequence the media coverage of conventions very often focuses on research on women
- Women are substantially represented (mostly by feminists) on major boards and committees of the APA and other professional organizations

Within the APA Division of the Psychology of Women, furthermore, serious steps, reflected in allocation of scarce resources, have been taken to ensure the participation of underrepresented groups (women of color, lesbians, women of various ethnic backgrounds) in the decisionmaking functions of the division and of the organization as a whole. The networks and bibliographic resources necessary to make research by and about black women and Hispanic women accessible to a wide audience of psychologists are now available, as are texts and material for integrating research in the psychology of women into traditional subfields of psychology.[4] Feminist women are also active and effective in most of the other APA divisions (APA has forty-seven divisions, each representing a specific area of psychology). Feminist groups have a voice in clinical psychology and psychoanalysis as well as in social, developmental, industrial/organizational, educational psychology, and so forth, and they work together with considerable political clout on issues arising within the organization as a whole.

It is clear there have been substantial changes in psychology as a result of feminism, and it is likely research will continue in the future to include women, feminist issues, and gender as topics incorporated into the general knowledge base in psychology,[5] if not into the awareness and thinking of individual psychologists. Despite these real and important changes, however, I think, as Stacey and Thorne[6] have argued for sociology, there is a missing feminist revolution in psychology. Women as subject matter and as professionals have been incorporated into—in the sense of grafted onto—psychology, but psychology has not been transformed in the sense usually meant by feminist scholars in the early days of enthusiastic self-consciousness about the enterprise.[7] In this sense, a transformation in psychology—a qualitative reshaping of the discipline—would result from putting experiences and activities of women at the center of the inquiry and shaping concepts, theories, and methods to articulate and provide an understanding of psychological phenomena from this perspective, rather than from the perspective traditionally adopted in psychology—that of socially privileged men. In addition to the reasons Stacey and Thorne discussed (all of which seem also to apply), I think there is an equally important and usually unnoted reason why feminism has not had an impact on psychology at a more fundamental conceptual/methodological level. Ultimately, the reason has to do with the way scientific psychology presently functions as part of the larger society.[8]

Psychology and the Science Model

In brief I think it can be argued that when psychological topics are formulated in traditional research paradigms, they are "deformed" in characteristic ways.[9] Psychological phenomena, events, processes are stripped of their socio-cultural, political, and personal meanings as they are reformulated to fit the concepts and theories permitted by the narrow range of research methods that are compatible with a positivist view of science. Through its privileging of a narrow range of methods[10] and the assumptions underlying them, psychology describes human activities in an ostensibly scientific language of a very particular kind for public discussion of social issues (including gender relations) and more subtly and pervasively for discussion of human beings in their relation to the social order. This language is one that (re)presents the individual not as an agent who acts for reasons in a social and moral order but as a being subjected in natural-law-like ways to various casual influences conceptualized as variables or factors. For example, people may "have perceptions of danger" but do not fear anyone, they may "have self-schemas" but are not selves. This is not a concise technical language that can be unpacked into statements about what people do and why; it is jargon that systematically obscures the actor and the reasons for acting through introduction of a scientistic terminology of cause and effect. To the extent that this representation of persons in mechanistic, agentless, nonmoral language becomes part of public discourse (or part of the discourse of the educated elites), it deprives the general public of the richer linguistic resources for self-interpretation and self-understanding inherent in the everyday language of persons, actions, reasons, motives, and values.[11] These resources enable or even encourage people to experience and think of themselves as agents who can act politically and in other ways in a world of meaning toward ends they value. The mechanistic, pseudoscientific language of psychology thus plays its role in the reproduction of the existing social order by pervading public discourse and the interpretations of ourselves that are shaped by it, displacing a discourse more compatible with the self-interpretations necessary for people to act together for social change.

If this is even a partly correct analysis of the relationship of the methods, concepts, and language of mainstream psychology, particularly social psychology, to the larger culture, it is not surprising that the subfields of psychology most relevant to an understanding of social phenomena have proved extremely resistant to the kinds of fundamental conceptual changes envisaged by (among others) feminists. The forces shaping psychology from "outside" the discipline and perpetuating it in its present form are powerful compared with forces for change from within.

Beyond Disciplinary Confines:
An Interdisciplinary Context

Mainstream psychology in practice defines itself not by subject matter but by a particular conception of method and the assumptions and language associated with it.[12] Therefore, psychologists who are intellectually and personally oriented both to problems in the real world and to scientific understanding typically either have to give up their problem and action focus as they and it become incorporated into mainstream psychology or have to create for themselves an interdisciplinary group of people with similar theoretical and practical interests.[13] Feminist psychologists are fortunate in not having to create *de novo* an interdisciplinary context for their work; it is already partly there in feminist scholarship as a body of literature and a community of scholars, both of which are as accessible as psychological literature and organizations of psychologists. An analysis of citation patterns in the literature, however, would probably confirm the impression of many who participate in interdisciplinary activities that feminist psychology and psychologists are relatively isolated from feminist scholarship in other disciplines.[14] The more puzzling question then would seem to be not why feminist psychologists have had relatively little impact on mainstream psychology but why feminist psychology and feminist work in other disciplines and in the interdisciplinary matrix of feminist theory appear to have so little relationship to one another.[15]

To begin to answer the latter question, it is worth noting that some of the psychological work best known to feminists outside psychology (most recently that of Carol Gilligan) has not been the focus of empirical research within psychology by feminists, primarily because the methods of traditional scientific psychology cannot be used to study it. However, some of the major topics in what is now the subfield called the psychology of women are conceptualized and researched in such a way that they appear to have had relatively little influence on or relationship to the work of feminist scholars in other disciplines. I want to show in what follows that Gilligan's work (as well as, for a second example, feminist psychological research on gender, language, and nonverbal communication) is compatible in its underlying assumptions with feminist research in other disciplines in a way more "mainstream" work on the psychology of women/gender probably is not. Further, Gilligan's work (and, more generally, feminist thinking about psychological phenomena) can be expanded and clarified in the interdisciplinary context of feminist scholarship and theory more fruitfully than it can by being adapted to the mainstream social psychological methods and language now used by many psychologists interested in women and in gender. As such, and in light of the foregoing argument about the role of the paradigms of mainstream psychology in the reproduction of the social order, an analysis of key features of Gilligan's work and of feminist research on gender and language may suggest directions for future research that provides genuine understanding of the psychological component of human activities and promotes social change.

A Challenge to Mainstream Psychology: The Work of Carol Gilligan

Carol Gilligan's research and writing have focused on three interrelated topics, all of which have both critical implications for traditional psychological theories and positive suggestions for future interdisciplinary feminist research. Some of her earlier and perhaps less well known work was a fundamental critique from a feminist perspective of psychological theories of adult development. Such theories, she pointed out, conceptualize psychological growth and maturity (or positively valued "development") primarily in terms of increasing autonomy and independence.[16] For many women, Gilligan noted, the reality of interdependency in relationships and a concomitant experience of connectedness with others might be more salient and more highly valued. Theories of psychological development in adulthood and notions of maturity need to include both separation and connectedness as do real people.

Gilligan's insights about the possibly differential importance of separation and connectedness in the lives of women and men are elaborated in the other two topics of her work: moral reasoning and the related phenomenon of the experience of oneself in relation to others.[17] As is by now common knowledge (though still not always reflected in the syllabi of courses or the bibliographies of papers on moral development), the heart of Gilligan's critique is that the dominant theory and method in research on moral development, that of Lawrence Kohlberg, incorporates the same gender-biased assumptions that distort theories of adult development. The highest stages of moral reasoning, according to Kohlberg's theory, involve reasoning with general moral principles that treat each individual as an abstract entity, interchangeable with any and all others. This highest level, Kohlberg found, was less often reached by women. Where Kohlberg implicitly finds defect in women's moral reasoning, however, Gilligan finds difference—if researchers will only listen. Analyzing women's reasoning in an actual moral dilemma (as opposed to the gender- and class-biased hypothetical vignettes Kohlberg employed), Gilligan found that the women in her study often reasoned in terms of principles applying not to abstracted, isolated individuals but to particular persons whose individuality is specified in part by their relationships to others. For these women, moral principles involved not rights of abstract, interchangeable individuals but responsibilities for caring for particular, interdependent others. She proposed that the kind of moral reasoning Kohlberg identified and studied, a rights-based morality of justice, needs to be supplemented with a conception of a morality of care based on empathic appreciation of the concrete situation of particular others. In other work, Gilligan and her colleagues have explored empirically the idea that women's predominant mode of moral reasoning (a morality of care) is related to their sense of themselves in relation to others.[18] For women, they have argued, the sense of self involves more connectedness with others than does men's (and separation is experienced as isolation and is frightening); men's sense of themselves involves greater separation from others than does women's (and closeness is experienced as engulfment and is frightening). Working with a coding scheme related to Gilligan's, Nona Lyons claimed her data show that such gender differences in the predominant mode of experiencing the self in relation to others are present from the teenage years through late middle age.

New Lines of Inquiry

In and through this work, Carol Gilligan clearly has provided an important corrective to a significant gender bias in theories of psychological development and theories of moral reasoning and of the self in traditional psychology. That it is not always acknowledged by traditional psychological researchers does not seriously diminish the importance of her theoretical contribution.[19] The central ideas arising from Gilligan's critique, however, have been and can fruitfully be developed not in mainstream psychology in exactly her terms, but at psychology's edges, at its boundaries with other disciplines.

It should be emphasized that this brief overview does not begin to do justice to the subtlety and complexity of the analyses of and commentaries on Gilligan's work that have come from scholars in disciplines other than psychology. Good examples of these—although they are of variable quality—can be found in the 1983 issue "Women and Morality" of *Social Research*, in the 1987 collection of papers and commentaries on women and moral development in *New Ideas in Psychology*, in the 1987 issue "Science, Morality, and Feminist Theory" of the *Canadian Journal of Philosophy*, in an article by S. Benhabib,[20] and in the volumes and articles cited in these works. As these critiques and commentaries have evolved, they have contributed to the development of—or resonate with, in ways that can be mutually enriching—feminist work in the history and philosophy of science[21] and in moral philosophical and political theory.[22] When mainstream psychologists have addressed Gilligan's work, however, a primary focus has been on the question of whether or not there are gender differences in any of the phenomena described.[23] (Other psychologists working more at the edges of mainstream research traditions have formulated more interesting questions vis-à-vis the issues Gilligan raises.)[24]

In addition to their intersection with moral philosophy and with feminist analyses of science—and moving in a different direction from most of the psychologists just mentioned—I think Gilligan's ideas might be usefully integrated with some of Dorothy Smith's work in sociology, particularly with ideas from Smith's classic analysis of what a sociology for women would look like.[25] Smith's work implicitly suggests that independence and autonomy might be qualities especially valued by and salient for one particular group in this society: those whose work and family roles are structured in such a way as to render essential support work of others culturally and psychologically invisible. Such individuals—usually men who have wives, secretaries, and sometimes platoons of other invisible (often female) presences or technologies behind their supposedly individual achievements—might understandably build theories that articulate and validate the public (ideological) version of their own experiences. However, psychological theories of development stressing autonomy, independence, and separateness may describe the development of the consciousness of individuals in particularly privileged social locations rather than the psychological reality of these individuals' actual situations or selves as persons in a social order. In other words, autonomy might not be a feature of an individual's personality (as traditional psychological theories would have it) or even the actual possibility of relatively unconstrained actions by individuals in particularly privileged social locations. Rather it might be a characteristic mode of awareness of one's dependence on others.

From this point of view, the psychological issues raised by Gilligan's work, when integrated with Smith's, have to do with the discovery and

analysis of differences between the ways some men and some women
come to experience (become conscious of) the forms of their connectedness
with others when some of their relationships of dependency are culturally
rendered both psychologically and ideologically invisible. This view is
partly implicit in Gilligan's writing, but combining her work with Smith's
shifts the emphasis in crucial ways by pointing to the role of social
structure and ideology in the constitution of an individual's awareness
of self and others. This formulation is related to and compatible with
Chodorow's description of psychodynamic development within a structured social order (of which more below), a description that has had a
major influence in interdisciplinary feminist theory.

The shift in emphasis that comes about when Gilligan's work is
integrated with that of feminist sociologist Dorothy Smith is, of course,
moving away from the traditional psychological question of whether
men and boys "are" more "independent" (or "field independent") than
girls and women. While even first-rate feminist psychologists such as
Maccoby and Jacklin perforce took the question of "sex differences"
seriously fifteen years ago[26] (when that was how the relevant subfield
of psychology formulated the issues), advances in feminist scholarship,
in some areas of psychology, and in the thinking of many feminist
psychologists have rendered the question moot for those interested in
a psychological understanding of gender. Research on sex differences—
now spoken of within the field as gender differences but not fundamentally
reconceptualized—has the same scientific interest as does, for example,
research on "age differences": that is, it has no interest in serious work
at the forefront on any particular psychological phenomenon. Thus most
developmental psychologists tacitly recognize that age is not a meaningful
variable and that focusing on age differences in, for example, problem
solving does not illuminate the psychological processes involved and
may not provide the most theoretically relevant articulation of comparison
groups for investigating the phenomenon of interest.

It is probably instructive to note that while developmental psychologists would not speak of age differences in the abstract, some
psychologists and most of the popular culture still speak of "sex
differences" without qualification (as to differences in what? Between
which women and which men?). The question of gender differences in
some particular phenomenon, I think, is one that retains its interest
among some psychologists not because it reasonably derives from a set
of scientific assumptions and data but because it is embedded in a
culturally compelling, essentially political, discourse about sex differences
and their origins in "nature" or "nurture." This framework is spoken
of in some subfields of psychology as the question of "how biological
and social factors interact," but the supposedly scientific formulation

essentially replicates that of public discourse. (The inadequacy and potential danger of operating from the "nature-nurture" frame has been well articulated by scholars from diverse disciplines.[27]) Given that the discourse shaping research in psychology is nonscientific and comes primarily from outside the field, it is perhaps not surprising that as Gilligan's work has been incorporated into mainstream psychology, the constitutive transactions between selves and social structure, which are in the foreground when Gilligan's work is integrated with Smith's, have faded into the background. The post-Gilligan question in psychology all too often continues to be whether girls and women "are" more "interdependent" and more "relational" than boys and men, whether they "are" different in level or type of moral reasoning.

The Notion of a "Self"

To further understand why Gilligan's work, particularly her work on the self, seems to be more compatible with and enriched by integration into disciplines other than psychology—and to understand also some of its limitations for feminist theory—it may be useful to consider her work in light of interdisciplinary work by social psychologists and others in Great Britain and Europe, which they call a "new psychology."[28] Part of this new psychology (and it is that vis-à-vis mainstream U.S. psychology) involves a revision of the image of human nature that is embedded in and perpetuated by psychological theories. In particular the new psychology rejects concepts and methods that implicitly conceptualize human beings as automata (beings that respond to causes rather than persons who act for reasons). The implicit conceptualization of persons as automata is currently introduced in mainstream U.S. psychology via the metaphor of person-as-computer or as an "information processing device."[29] (When behaviorism was the dominant perspective in psychology, persons were implicitly conceptualized as automata that "respond" to "stimuli" in the environment; now, after the "cognitive revolution," persons are implicitly conceptualized as automata that "process" "information" in the environment.)

The notion of a self, when formulated as a topic for empirical research, has proved difficult for U.S. psychologists to conceptualize in nonmechanistic terms.[30] Typically, the self is treated as an entity that is "perceived" (as in "self-perception") or something (a "self-schema") that is "had" in the sense of "owned" by some unspecified agent. A stimulus-response, cause-and-effect model or a model of a master computer program manipulating lower-level information processing modules prevails over a conceptualization of persons as active interpreters, makers of meaning. Part of the appeal of Gilligan's work to many feminist psychologists is that it uses everyday language for talking about selves and thereby implies the possibility of a richer conception of the human person—as someone who seeks/makes meaning in a social and moral order, an agent who actively interprets and transforms the world according to the needs and purposes inherent in practical activities. The latter view of human nature is of course assumed by scholars in the humanities as well as by most laypeople. Differences between a view of persons as agents and the mechanistic conception currently dominating U.S. psychology, including much feminist psychology, is probably the most important single reason for the gap in communication between feminist psychologists and feminist scholars in other disciplines. Because the politically and morally grounded European social psychologists explicitly reject the image of people as automata and have begun to develop appropriate new methods of investigation, I think their works represent a promising theoretical and empirical framework within which feminist psychology can develop (be transformed).

Thinking about Gilligan's work on the self in the context of the new psychology, for example, might lead to a surprising reformulation. Although they do not represent a single view, some psychologists involved in the new psychology (most notably Rom Harre) draw on the considerable cultural variation in conceptions of the self[31] to argue that for theoretical purposes the self is most fruitfully regarded not as an entity with attributes but as a locally specific theory that social actors acquire in order to participate in a particular way in the discourses in which they are engaged. In this view we do not so much "have" an inner, private self that has particular properties and that "causes" our actions as we hold a theory of self that allows us to make self-ascriptions (as in the avowal of an emotional state) and to otherwise participate in discourse in certain ways.[32] This way of thinking of selves as socially constituted in language, of subjectivity as constructed via a semiotic discourse, represents an ontological shift from the view of the self as a schema or property of a material being. It begins to connect in a way that conceptions of "self-perceptions" and "self-schemas" do not with concerns about subjectivity and language as they have arisen in feminist literary and film criticism and in certain kinds of discourse analysis.[33]

In addition to its implicit conception of the person as agent, then, Gilligan's work can be seen as pointing to a second key assumption that may separate most feminist psychologists from feminist scholars in other disciplines: an assumption about the relationship of individual selves/subjectivity and the social order. Feminist scholars in disciplines other than psychology have drawn on Gilligan's work with unusual enthusiasm, in part because it is almost universally read by feminists against a theoretical background previously laid out by Dorothy

Dinnerstein[34] and especially by Nancy Chodorow.[35] Chodorow's work, central in feminist theory, persuasively argued for the necessity of a description of personality in sociologically grounded psychodynamic terms as central to an understanding of the ongoing reproduction of gender (the continuation of the social relations of gender from generation to generation).[36] Chodorow's work explicitly and strongly emphasized the dialectical, mutually constituting relationship between individual personality and social order. Like the "new" social psychologists, and very unlike traditional psychologists in the United States, her starting point was the social order, and she asked how individuals come into being as persons within it. For the reader with Chodorow in mind, then, Gilligan's description of gendered personalities offers a fuller characterization (with a focus on the individual) of a dialectical process necessarily manifested only in historically and culturally particular social arrangements of childrearing.

Activity Theory

Brinton Lykes has suggested that Gilligan's work, even when read in the context of Chodorow, does not completely escape the assumptions of autonomous individualism she critiques in Kohlberg.[37] Although Gilligan's work is based on a conception of the person as an agent (and although this agent is not conceptualized with a masculine bias), Lykes argued that the underlying notion of self is still fundamentally that of a separate entity who interacts with (is connected with or related to) another separate entity. In this respect Gilligan has simply provided a "'female' variation of the dominant 'male' model of the egocentric contractual idea of the self."[38] Social relations, and by extension the social order, are reduced in this conceptualization (which Popper called "methodological psychologism"[39]) to interactions among individuals analytically conceived (and methodologically investigated) in asocial terms. The key feature of the social order—that it is structured, that individuals are differently located in it—is rendered invisible (or at least inconspicuous) by the persistence of the assumptions of autonomous individualism.[40]

What is needed instead, Lykes said, is a psychological approach that takes as its starting point not the individual person but human activities— a unit of analysis that includes both the individual and her or his culturally defined environment as a dynamic, mutually constituting system. It is within human activities that the individuality of persons is articulated (comes into being) in relationships. Like Chodorow, Lykes thus connected the formation of selves with the particularities of social location, but her use of activity theory makes more explicit ways in which persons actively transform their worlds as they are formed by them. The conceptualization of the self as an individual, materially embodied entity is replaced in Lykes's work by the notion of "social individuality" which has meaning only as an articulation of a mutually constituting relationship of self and social order. It is very difficult, as Lykes pointed out, to hold consistently the dialectical conception of social individuality in the face of habits of language use that describe the self in the terms of an ideology of autonomous individualism. The great virtue of Lykes's work, apart from its originality in contemporary terms and its connections with earlier, now-neglected traditions in psychology (Mead, H. S. Sullivan), is that it is grounded within a thriving theoretical perspective and body of empirical work known as activity theory.[41] Unlike the works of Gilligan and Kohlberg, which at bottom rest on a conceptualization of the individual as separable from and prior to the social order, programmatic empirical exploration of social individuality can be readily undertaken within the tradition of activity theory. I think it represents a promising direction for future research by feminist psychologists who want to see their work integrated with feminist scholarship in other disciplines and who want to develop transformed psychological knowledge that is useful for social change.

The Popularity of Gilligan's Work

Apart from its particular contributions to psychology and to feminist scholarship in other disciplines, what is most striking about Gilligan's work is the reaction to it both by academics and by popular audiences and professions outside the academy. A great many women say that the "different voice" Gilligan hears in women's moral reasoning (the focus on particulars of a person and situation, the it-depends-on-the-circumstances reluctance to reason with general principles about abstract entities) is one they know from their own experience but had never heard publicly articulated and validated before.[42] The response is like the less widespread but similarly heartfelt reaction to Chodorow's and Dinnerstein's earlier descriptions of a related phenomenon (women's sense of a continuing connectedness with and awareness of others) and to Jean Baker Miller's more recent elaboration from a clinical perspective.[43] The fact that Gilligan's work speaks truth in some significant sense does not mean, of course, that we understand the social and cultural meaning of the popularity of her work. Her description of gender differences is not all that different from descriptions of women's special qualities that some feminists (and nonfeminists) have offered in the past, although unlike feminists in the late 1960s, Gilligan does not simultaneously call for the social and cultural changes necessary to revalue, to really value, the qualities associated in this culture with some females. So why is Gilligan's work so popular now? As Pauline Bart said in a slightly different but related context,[44] we need to ask *cui bono?* Who benefits from this way of talking about gender? How can we explain the fact that the potentially harmful and destructive aspects of connectedness are so rarely named and explored?[45] How can we explain the fact that Gilligan's work has been taken up by men and by women in various educational settings with such extraordinary rapidity? (At the state level, for example, officials in New York formed a committee to consider the implications of this work for curriculum revisions; it has already been incorporated into the ethics curriculum in at least one private school in New York City; feminist theologians use Gilligan's work as do at least some social work educators.) There has been an unprecedentedly rapid diffusion of Gilligan's ideas from academic psychology to what are sometimes called applied settings. Something is going on, having to do with the shaping of and control over the public discourse about gender. This phenomenon is worthy of investigation in its own right by feminist scholars apart from the use of the substantive content of Gilligan's work in their research. A significant feature of Gilligan's work may shed light on the ease and speed with which it has been "adopted": Although it uses the language of agents rather than automata to describe human beings, it nevertheless implicitly retains a central assumption of mainstream psychology in (re)presenting the individual as conceptually separable from and prior to the social order. Rather than providing a challenge or corrective to the culturally powerful ideology of autonomous individualism, Gilligan's work is capable of being assimilated into and interpreted as scientific support for the public, political discourse about gender (as "gender differences" and what are implicitly assumed to be their biological or social causes).

Gender, Communication, and the Social Order

Analysis of feminist research on language, gender, and nonverbal communication[46] further underscores the significance of assumptions about the individual and the social order for the development of psychological knowledge that can be integrated with and enriched by feminist research and scholarship in other disciplines. As is the case in Chodorow's work, in the "new" social psychology, and in Dorothy Smith's kind of sociology, the starting point in feminist work on language, gender, and nonverbal communication is the structured social order, and the focus is on transactions between persons acting as agents within it. In this research, language use and nonverbal modes of communication are conceptualized as a means through which individuals create and recreate relations of dominance in the social order.[47] A paradigmatic example is Henley's[48] research on touching: When observations are made of occasions when one person touches another (in contexts where it does not clearly have a sexual or affectionate meaning), the pattern of touching between individuals is often nonreciprocal; the person in a socially dominant position is the one who touches a social subordinate, but not vice versa. Henley described touching in such situations as a covert (and deniable) assertion of power or dominance by the person who touches. If the assertion is implicitly confirmed or acknowledged by the other's response (when the subordinate permits the touch and does not reciprocate), then a relationship of dominance is created in the face-to-face interaction relationship that recreates (affirms, maintains, perpetuates) the power relationships at the macrosocial level. In the theoretical framework guiding this research, power is not something an individual "has" or an attribute of their personality. It is a shared meaning created in a mutually confirming transaction between two persons, both of whom have to play their part for that particular meaning to emerge. What such an analysis illuminates, of course, is the active role of both persons in creating power and dominance, in recreating the macrosocial relations and structures of dominance through microsocial processes of transactions. From a feminist perspective, such an analysis is particularly important because it demonstrates significant circumstances in which women are not passive victims of their situation but can act as agents to alter the transaction and to create new meanings. In Henley's analysis, the links between social structure, individual agents, social meaning, and social changes are made very clear—in a way Chodorow's work partly illuminates and Gilligan's much less so.

In addition to nonverbal gestures, several other gender-related phenomena have been examined from the theoretical perspective outlined by Thorne and Henley (a perspective compatible with and increasingly integrated with ethnographic and other research on social identity and language use[49]). For example,[50] nonreciprocal use of the other person's first name (as opposed to title plus last name) has been shown to be related to the relative status or power of two people in an interaction. Interruptions—disruption of smooth exchange of conversational turns—have also been extensively investigated as gender-related phenomena. Candace West and Don Zimmerman[51] found that in many different kinds of settings, in conversations between friends or strangers, women are overwhelmingly more likely to be interrupted by men than men are by women. Similarly, Fishman[52] has shown that the topic of conversations was overwhelmingly more likely to be determined by men than by women. In her recordings of talk between couples over long periods of time, Fishman found that conversational topics introduced by the men were almost always followed up by their female partners, whereas topics introduced by women often were dropped when no response (or only minimal response—"umhum") was forthcoming. As had previously been demonstrated for interruptions, Fishman found that the women did *not* passively accept their role in the conversation, but actively made efforts to engage their partner in conversation on topics they wanted to discuss. Devices like tag questions (do you think?) and introductory questions (guess what?) were repeatedly used by the women to keep their topic going—without conspicuous success. The men, however, simply did not have to engage in this kind of conversational work to discuss a topic they were interested in.

Although more recent research points to the need to qualify generalizations about "men" and "women" (which men? which women? under what circumstances?), it is also clear that "conversational politics" of this sort[53] is a phenomenon that many women immediately recognize from their own experience. But I would suggest that unlike Gilligan's work, which also evokes such recognition, this research does not incorporate the assumption that the individual and the social order are conceptually separable—and that the social order does or should reflect the characteristics of individuals as described in the context—stripping people from their social context. It is a very different thing to assume, as do researchers in the tradition Thorne and Henley represent, that persons act as agents (in circumstances not of their own making) to create and recreate the social order: This assumption both recognizes the reality that gender is a principle of social organization and shows how people can act to change it. A recent elaboration of this theoretical perspective is the landmark paper "Doing Gender" by West and Zimmerman.[54] In this paper the authors analyzed gender as a feature of social organization that is continually reproduced through the activities of persons: Gender is a practical accomplishment in situated human activities, not a property or mode of personality organization of an individual. In this view, gender (including the gendered social order) is continually made and remade in the flow of human activities; it is not a static property (either in the individual or in a social role) that casually influences these activities from the outside. Like Lykes's research and the theoretical perspective she represents, the tradition represented by West and Zimmerman and by Thorne, Kramarae, and Henley presents a clear model of a direction feminist psychologists could go in the future if they want to work with assumptions (about the person as agent and about the relation of persons and the social order) that enable their research both to be integrated with feminist work in other disciplines and with feminist theory and also contribute to a public discourse about gender that will support rather than suppress social change.

A New View of Gender

It is worth emphasizing that the theoretical perspective embodied in feminist work on language, gender, and nonverbal communication is simply incommensurable with the traditional psychological notion of gender as an attribute or mode of functioning or content of the "social cognition" of an individual conceptualized and measured asocially. This is true both in terms of methods and in terms of the interpretation of data. For example, use of a "sex-role inventory" or other questionnaires as a method of investigation directed toward learning more about the individual will not capture—indeed, will preclude and will deform in characteristic ways—the phenomena involved in "doing gender" because those phenomena are mutually constituted meaningful transactions between persons rather than intrapersonal traits or responses to stimuli or ways of "processing information." Conceptions of personality in terms of traits (gender-associated or not, in the belief systems of the investigator or of those studied) are highly problematic, and the implications of these problems are considerable for mainstream psychological research on gender. Simply on semantic grounds it is clear that "aggression," for example, refers to something happening between two or more people; the word cannot meaningfully be used to describe an individual without reference to context. As an analytic concept in psychology, as opposed to an uncritical importation into psychology of popular talk, phenomena picked out by ordinary language as "aggression" occur between particular persons, under particular circumstances, and for reasons that need to be specified. In what can be seen as a linking of the notion of gender-associated "traits" or beliefs about them (or in contemporary terms "gender schema") with the conceptualization of gender as a practical accomplishment, Maltz and Borker[55] have suggested that some of the ways a person thinks about differences in personality traits between men and women might be a (culturally/ideologically shaped) interpretation of what are in effect the situated, gender-creating transactional phenomena West and Zimmerman described. Women might be thought to be more "concerned about other people" and more "tactful" than men, for example, because—*in settings where they want to accomplish certain goals and believe they can do so through particular linguistic strategies*—they ask their male conversational partner what he thinks; they talk about topics he is interested in. Men might be interpreted as being more "decisive" and "confident" than women because they speak—again, strategically and purposefully—without interruptions. What Maltz and Borker are pointing to in their sociolinguistic analysis, then, is the possibility that trait descriptions of personality represent culturally shaped, abstract generalizations

inferred from typical patterns of situated, meaningful, goal-directed interactions. These abstractions are inferred from situated activities of
persons but are characteristically (in this culture) conceptualized as personality traits and attributed to a (decontextualized) individual, thereby
ideologically obscuring the meanings of the transactions for the participants—and the way they recreate and reproduce a gendered social order.
The challenge to feminists is to illuminate this ideological function, not
work with concepts and methods that support and perpetuate it.

Conclusion

I have tried to show in this chapter that, as examples of feminist
psychology that can be integrated with and enriched by feminist scholarship in other disciplines, analysis of Gilligan's work and of research
on gender, language, and nonverbal communication highlights the importance of two issues about which assumptions are necessarily made
in psychological research and theory. One is the conception of the person
(as agent or as automata) that is implicit in the concepts and methods
of research. The other is the conceptualization and methods for investigating the person in relation to the social order. I believe that a clearer
and more consistent commitment to a conception of agency and to a
conception of social activity as the starting point for psychological
analysis will be helpful—indeed essential—if feminist psychological
research is to be integrated with feminist scholarship in other disciplines
and to lead to knowledge that is useful for understanding and social
change. I have tried to suggest that to the extent that feminists use
paradigms—methods and concepts and language—of traditional psychology that implicitly (re)present the person as an automaton and the
social order as arising from interactions among (fundamentally asocial)
individuals, feminist psychological work has been and will be incorporated
into mainstream psychology and has been and will be isolated from
feminist scholarship in other disciplines. It seems to me this situation
is not politically or morally neutral, because feminist psychology that
adopts mainstream psychology's methods and concepts and language is
likely to reproduce or at least leave unchallenged the ideological discourses
that justify and recreate the social relations of gender.[56]

Notes

1. D. L. Fowlkes and C. S. McClure, eds., *The Genesis of Feminist Visions
for Transforming the Liberal Arts Curriculum* (Birmingham: University of Alabama
Press, 1984); E. C. DuBois et al., eds., *Feminist Scholarship: Kindling the Groves*

of Academe (Urbana: University of Illinois Press, 1985); M. Parlee, "Psychology: Review essay," *Signs* 1(1975):119–131; M. Parlee, "Psychology and Women: Review essay," *Signs* 5(1979):121–133; M. Parlee, "Psychology of Women in the 80s: Promising problems," *International Journal of Women's Studies* 8(1985):193–204.

2. American Psychological Association, *Publication Manual*, 3rd. ed. (Washington, D.C.: American Psychological Association, 1984).

3. F. Denmark, N. F. Russo, I. H. Frieze, and J. A. Sechzer, "Guidelines for Avoiding Sexism in Psychological Research," *American Psychologist* 43(1988):582–585.

4. P. Bronstein and K. Quina, eds., *Teaching the Psychology of People: Resources for Gender and Sociocultural Awareness* (Washington, D.C.: American Psychological Association, 1988); M. Paludi, *Exploring/Teaching the Psychology of Women: A Manual of Resources* (Albany: SUNY Press, 1988).

5. K. Deau, "From Individual Differences to Social Categories: Analysis of a decade's research on gender," *American Psychologist* 39(1984):105–116; M. Fine, "Reflections on a Feminist Psychology of Women: Paradoxes and prospects," *Psychology of Women Quarterly* 9(1985):167–183.

6. J. Stacey and B. Thorne, "The Missing Feminist Revolution in Psychology," *Social Problems* 32(1985):319–316.

7. M. J. Boxer, "For and About Women: The theory and practice of women's studies in the United States," *Signs* 7(1982):661–695; Du Bois et al., *Feminist Scholarship*. In psychology, see B. S. Wallston, "What are the Questions in the Psychology of Women: A feminist approach to research," *Psychology of Women Quarterly* 5(1981):597–617 and M. A. Wittig, "Meta-theoretical Dilemmas in the Psychology of Gender," *American Psychologist* 40(1985):800–811.

8. C. W. Sherif, "Bias in Psychology," in *The Prism of Sex: Essays on the Sociology of Knowledge*, ed. J. A. Sherman and F. T. Beck (Madison: University of Wisconsin Press, 1979).

9. M. Parlee, "Psychology and Women"; M. Parlee, "Appropriate Control Groups in Feminist Research," *Psychology of Women Quarterly* 5(1981):637–644.

10. M. B. Lykes and A. J. Stewart, "Evaluating the Feminist Challenge to Research in Personality and Social Psychology: 1963–1983," *Psychology of Women Quarterly* 10(1986):393–412.

11. R. Harre, *Personal Being* (Cambridge, Mass.: Harvard University Press, 1984); R. Harre, "An Analysis of Social Activity," in *States of Mind*, ed. J. Miller (New York: Pantheon, 1983).

12. K. Danziger, "The Methodological Imperative in Psychology," *Philosophy of the Social Sciences* 32(1985):301–316.

13. There is nothing unique to feminists about this situation. Environmental psychology is a field that faced such a choice several years ago, as did health psychology and feminist psychology.

14. M. Parlee, "Happy Birthday to *Feminism and Psychology!*" *Feminism and Psychology* 1(1991):39–48. This isolation is in part a result of feminists' organizational "success" in becoming absorbed into the methodological paradigms of various mainstreams of psychology (social psychology, clinical psychology,

educational psychology, and so forth). As the research proceeds, feminists have become specialized in the way most psychologists are specialized (why specialize this way is the question I raise here), which means we tend to lose touch with each other and with a coherent identity both as feminist psychologists and as part of the broader enterprise of feminist scholarship. For reasons at the heart of the intersection of politics and knowledge, we need that coherent identity in order to be able to develop and implement in organizational terms new criteria of excellence—a new definition of what constitutes good psychological research, thinking, practice.

15. One of the great dangers this isolation poses for intellectual life and for political change informed by research and theory is that of throwing out the baby with the bathwater. Although many feminist scholars and activists rightly disregard psychological research based on methodological individualism and focused on persons (as "subjects") stripped from their social and physical contexts, there is the danger that they might mistake this framework and these results for all that psychological analysis has to offer. Feminist psychologists, however, unnecessarily limit their methods and conceptual frameworks (and audiences) when they use methods from mainstream psychology that reformulate psychological phenomena into a mechanistic language that is inadequate for the complexity of the phenomena and incompatible with the interpretive understanding that is the goal of the humanities and some of the social sciences. See J. Stacey and B. Thorne, "The Missing Feminist Revolution," 310–316.) The relevance of an approach that focuses on the differences between disciplines seeking causal explanations and those seeking interpretive understanding is underscored by V. R. Hyman, "Conflict and Contradictions: Principles of feminist scholarship," *Academic Questions* Winter(1987–1988):5–14, in a discussion of the impact of feminism on traditional disciplines. Hyman also thinks the distinction is important but, unlike Stacey and Thorne and myself, believes feminism has succeeded in changing disciplines that seek causal explanations but has not succeeded in its aim of "transform[ing] a political position into a scholarly pursuit" in disciplines that seek interpretive understanding.

16. Levinson's discussion of a stage at midlife called "Becoming One's Own Man" is notable only for its truth in packaging; Erikson's conceptualization of an "identity crisis" in late adolescence puts similar emphasis on separation and independence as a prerequisite for the development of satisfactory adult relationships.

17. C. Gilligan, "In a Different Voice: Women's conception of self and morality," *Harvard Educational Review* 47(1977):481–517; C. Gilligan, "Restoring the Missing Text of Women's Development to Life Cycle Theories," in *Women's Lives: New Theory, Research, Policy,* ed. D. C. McGuigan (Ann Arbor: University of Michigan Center for Continuing Education of Women, 1980); C. Gilligan, *In a Different Voice: Psychological Theory and Women's Development* (Cambridge, Mass.: Harvard University Press, 1982); C. Gilligan and J. M. Murphy, "Development from Adolescence to Adulthood: The philosopher and the dilemma of the fact," in *Intellectual Development Beyond Childhood,* ed. D. Kuhn (San Francisco: Jossey-Bass, 1979); J. M. Murphy and C. Gilligan, "Moral Development

in Late Adolescence: A critique and reconstruction of Kohlberg's theory," *Human Development* 23(1980):77–104.

18. N. Lyons, "Two Perspectives on Self, Relationships, and Morality," *Harvard Educational Review* 53(1983):125–145; S. Pollack and C. Gilligan, "Images of Violence in Thematic Apperception Test Stories," *Journal of Personality and Social Psychology* 42(1982):159–167.

19. One recent major research program in children's social development, for example, explicitly differentiates moral reasoning (used in Kohlberg's sense) from reasoning about what are called "personal concerns" (loyalty to family members over strangers, for example). This resort to a stipulative definition of morality (in effect, defining it by stating it in a loud voice and simply ignoring the issues Gilligan raises) suggests that the bias in concepts and values that Gilligan has identified is very important indeed, as do the vitriolic—one might almost say shrill—attacks that have been made on her by some traditional psychologists and philosophers. See J. M. Broughton, "Women's Rationality and Men's Virtue: A critique of gender dualism in Gilligan's theory of moral development," *Social Research* 50(1983):597–642; J. C. Walker, "In a Different Voice: Cryptoseparatist Analysis of Female Moral Development," *Social Research* 50(1983):665–695.

20. S. Benhabib, "The Generalized and the Concrete Other: The Kohlberg-Gilligan controversy and feminist theory," in *Feminism as Critique: On the Politics of Gender,* ed. S. Benhabib and O. Cornell (Minneapolis: University of Minnesota Press, 1987), 77–95.

21. S. Harding and J. F. O'Barr, *Sex and Scientific Inquiry* (Chicago: University of Chicago Press, 1987); E. F. Keller, *Reflections on Gender and Science* (New Haven: Yale University Press, 1985).

22. V. Held, "Changing Perspectives in Philosophy," Chapter 2 of this volume; E. F. Kittay and D. T. Meyers, *Women and Moral Theory* (Totowa, N.J.: Rowman and Littlefield, 1987).

23. M. Brabeck, "Moral Development: Theory and research on differences between males and females," *Developmental Review* 3(1983):274–291; J. Fishkin, K. Keniston, and C. MacKinnon, "Moral Reasoning and Political Ideology," *Journal of Personality and Social Psychology* 27(1983):109–119; L. J. Walker, "Sex Differences in the Development of Moral Reasoning: A critical review," *Child Development* 55(1984):677–691.

24. N. Haan, "An Interactional Morality of Everyday Life," in *Social Science as Moral Inquiry,* ed. N. Haan, P. Rabinow, and W. Sullivan (New York: Columbia University Press, 1983); A. H. Bloom and J. Marecek, "The Dual Role of Dialogue in Moral Development: A response to Philibert," *New Ideas in Psychology* 5(1987):233–238.

25. D. Smith, "A Sociology for Women," in *The Prism of Sex: Essays on the Sociology of Knowledge,* ed. J. A. Sherman and E. T. Beck (Madison: University of Wisconsin Press, 1979).

26. E. E. Maccoby and C. N. Jacklin, *The Psychology of Sex Differences* (Stanford: Stanford University Press, 1974).

27. T. de Lauretis, *Technologies of Gender: Essays on Theory, Film and Fiction* (Bloomington: Indiana University Press, 1987); E. F. Keller, "On the Need to

Count Past Two in Our Thinking about Gender and Science," *New Ideas in Psychology* 5(1987):275–288. Both Keller, a scientist/historian, and de Lauretis, a film critic, have given rich and cogent analyses of the empirical inadequacy and the negative political consequences for women of accepting this "biology/ environment" dichotomy as the basis of feminist inquiry. Rachel Hare-Mustin, a clinical psychologist, made a related argument in a way and in a forum more likely to be accessible to psychologists: R. T. Hare-Mustin, "The Gender Dichotomy and Developmental Theory: A response to Sayers," *New Ideas in Psychology* 5(1987):261–265.

28. R. Harre, O. Clarke, and N. de Carlo, *Motives and Mechanism: An Introduction to the Psychology of Action* (New York: Methuen, 1985).

29. Feminist psychology also seems to be becoming absorbed into this paradigm as feminist psychology/the psychology of gender/social psychology become increasingly amalgamated. See B. Lott, "The Potential Enrichment of Social/personality Psychology through Feminist Research and Vice Versa," *American Psychologist* 40(1985):155–164 and R. K. Unger, "Epilogue: Toward a synthesis of women, gender and social psychology," in *Women, Gender and Social Psychology*, ed. V. E. O'Leary, R. K. Unger, and B. S. Wallston (Hillsdale: Erlbaum, 1985), 349–358, for more positive views than I have of this development. Sandra Bem's earlier work on gender schema theory, for example, is based on the "information processing" metaphor currently dominating social psychological research on "social cognition" (S. L. Bem, "Gender Schema Theory and the Romantic Tradition," in *Sex and Gender: Review of Personality and Social Psychology*, vol. 7, ed. P. Shaver and C. Hendrick [Newbury Park, Calif.: Sage, 1986]:251–271) as is feminist research on the self (H. Markus, M. Crane, S. Bernstein, and M. Siladi, "Self-schemas and Gender," *Journal of Personality and Social Psychology* 42[1982]:38–50) and on the psychology of menstruation (D. N. Ruble and J. Brooks-Sunn, "Menstrual Symptoms: A social cognitive analysis of perception of symptoms," *Journal of Behavioral Medicine* 2[1979]:171–194). I have argued elsewhere that the "social cognition" paradigm (the interrelated set of methods, language, concepts, assumptions) is inadequate at least for understanding the psychological concomitants of the menstrual cycle (M. Parlee, "Menstrual Cycle Changes in Moods and Emotions: Causal and interpretive processes in the construction of emotions," in *Social Psychophysiology and Emotion: Theory and Clinical Applications*, ed. H. Wagner (Chichester: Wiley, 1988).

30. H. Markus and K. Sentis, "The Self in Social Information Processing," in *Psychological Perspectives on the Self*, ed. J. Suls (Hillsdale: Erlbaum, 1981).

31. R. A. Shweder and R. A. Levine, *Culture Theory: Essays on Mind, Self, and Emotion* (New York: Cambridge University Press, 1984).

32. Harre, *Personal Being*.

33. See L. Alcoff, "Cultural Feminism vs. Post-structuralism: The identity crisis in feminist theory," *Signs* 13(1988):405–436.

34. D. Dinnerstein, *The Mermaid and the Minotaur: Sexual Arrangements and Human Malaise* (New York: Harper and Row, 1976).

35. N. Chodorow, *The Reproduction of Mothering* (Berkeley: University of California Press, 1978).

36. In *The Reproduction of Mothering*, Chodorow argued that the social arrangements whereby women mother both girls and boys—particularly in the nuclear family—are integrally related to the sexual division of labor in the workplace. It is through particular forms of socially organized childrearing that individuals are produced (as she put it) with the psychological dispositions (the capacities, motivations, abilities) that are necessary to reproduce existing social relations of gender in the family and in the workplace. She discussed these psychological dispositions and their development in terms of object relations theory, with separation/individuation being central to adult gender differences in, among other things, the phenomenal experience of relatedness to others. (Despite the universality implied by some of Chodorow's language, there has been considerable discussion of the limitations of her description to middle-class nuclear families in Western industrialized societies, and her work is probably best read with this limitation in mind.)

37. M. B. Lykes, "Gender and Individualistic vs. Collectivist Based Notions about the Self," *Journal of Personality* 53(1985):356–383.

38. Ibid., 361.

39. K. R. Popper, *The Logic of Scientific Discovery* (New York: Basic Books, 1959).

40. J. Margolis, "The Middle Ground in Social Psychology," *New Ideas in Psychology* 5(1987):313–317 offers a brief but spirited critique of this perspective.

41. L. S. Vygotsky, *Mind in Society: The Development of Higher Psychological Processes* (Cambridge, Mass.: Harvard University Press, 1979); J. V. Wertsch, trans. and ed., *The Concept of Activity in Societ Psychology* (White Plains, N.Y.: Sharpe, 1981); S. Scribner, "Thinking in Action: Some characteristics of practical action," in *Practical Intelligence*, ed. R. J. Sternberg and R. K. Wagner (New York: Cambridge University Press, 1986).

42. It is an empirical question whether the click of recognition is to be found primarily among white, educated, middle-class women or whether the response is widespread among more diverse groups of women as Gilligan's unqualified descriptions of "women" implies.

43. J. Miller, *The Development of Women's Sense of Self* (Wellesley: Stone Center for Developmental Services and Studies at Wellesley College, Work-In-Progress Series, 1984).

44. P. Bart, "The Mermaid and the Minotaur: A fishy story that's part bull," review of D. Dinnerstein's *The Mermaid and the Minotaur*, *Contemporary Psychology* (1977):834–835.

45. J. Flax, "The Conflict Between Nurturance and Autonomy in Mother-Daughter Relationships and Within Feminism," *Feminist Studies* 4(1978):171–191, is a pre-Gilligan exception.

46. N. M. Henley, *Body Politics: Power, Sex, and Nonverbal Communication* (Englewood Cliffs: Prentice-Hall, 1977); B. Thorne and N. M. Henley, eds., *Language and Sex: Difference and Dominance* (Rowley, Mass.: Newbury House Publishers, 1975); B. Thorne, C. Kramarae, and N. M. Henley, eds., *Language, Gender and Society* (New York: Harper and Row, 1983).

47. B. Thorne and N. M. Henley, "Difference and Dominance: An overview of language, gender and society," in *Language and Sex: Difference and Dominance,*

ed. B. Thorne and N. M. Henley (Rowley, Mass.: Newbury House Publishers, 1975); see also R. Hodge and G. Kress, *Social Semiotics* (Ithaca, N.Y.: Cornell University Press, 1988).

48. N. M. Henley, "Power, Sex, and Nonverbal Communication," *Berkeley Journal of Sociology* 18(1973/74):1–26.

49. For example, J. J. Gumperz, *Language and Social Identity* (New York: Cambridge University Press, 1982).

50. Thorne and Henley, "Difference and Dominance," in *Language and Sex: Difference and Dominance*, ed. Thorne and Henley; Thorne, Kramarae, and Henley, *Language, Gender and Society*.

51. C. West and D. Zimmerman, "Doing Gender," *Gender and Society* 1(1987):125–151.

52. P. M. Fishman, "Interaction: The work women do," *Social Problems* 25(1978):397–406.

53. M. Parlee, "Conversational Politics," *Psychology Today*, May 1979.

54. West and Zimmerman, "Doing Gender."

55. D. N. Maltz and R. A. Borker, "A Cultural Approach to Male-female Miscommunication," in *Language and Social Identity*, ed. Gumperz, 195–216.

56. Given the power and pervasiveness of the cultural and economic forces that shape and form the content and future directions of psychology from the outside, feminist psychologists' most productive and enriching alliances in the future undoubtedly lie with feminist scholars in other disciplines. Now that feminists have acquired at least some of the organizational base necessary to define new criteria for what constitutes excellence in psychological research, we can use it to redefine and transform feminist psychology by giving greater priority not to persuasion of and argument with mainstream psychologists but to an expanded and fruitful dialogue with other feminist scholars. Quite concretely, this dialogue might begin in two ways: (1) Editors and reviewers could screen articles submitted for publication to ensure that they include references to and enter into substantive dialogue with the ideas in scholarly work in at least one discipline outside psychology; (2) Editors could set a strict limit (perhaps 50 percent to start) on the proportion of articles they publish in which questionnaires are the only method used for collection of data.

4
FEMINISM
AND SOCIOLOGY

INTRODUCTION: THE SEARCH FOR A FEMINIST/WOMANIST METHODOLOGY IN SOCIOLOGY
Susan A. Farrell

Feminist sociologists have sought to integrate feminism into sociology in a variety of ways. In addition to studying feminism as a social movement, feminist sociologists have also attempted to transform the discipline[1] and the way sociological research is done. Following a critical tradition in sociology that includes C. Wright Mills's[2] attention to the limitations of the scientific method and the problem of abstracted empiricism, Garfinkel's[3] ethnomethodological approach, a criticism of the unexamined assumptions about everyday life that ground sociological work, theory, and methods, and the Frankfurt School's critique of the pervasiveness of dominant ideologies[4] coupled with Foucault's analysis that alternative knowledges are suppressed and marginalized,[5] feminist researchers are also taking a long, hard look at sociological methods.

Sociology as an Objective Science

The scientific method with its concepts of objectivity as an Archimedean vantage point of detachment and abstraction, particularly as it has been used in quantitative sociological methods, screens out women's knowledge and experience of the world. Experience becomes homogenized and static. Rigid, unexamined categories do not allow for the fluidity or the messiness of day-to-day lived experience. Moreover, as a number of critics have demonstrated, these research methods are neither neutral nor objective.[6] They actually reflect men's attempts to understand and grasp their social situation, thus rendering women invisible[7] and universalizing the experience of white Euro-American middle- and upper-class men as definitive of human experience. Much research has failed to distinguish the varied experiences of women and men in social institutions and structures according to class, race-ethnicity, sexuality, geographical location, and other variables as well as gender.

Gender has not always been included as a unit of analysis nor made explicit in sociological research. Even when used as a category, it is often dismissed in the findings as irrelevant or too complicated to deal with in quantitative studies or relegated to a sentence or two whose implications are never explored.

Research on topics that explicitly required consideration of gender as a variable is fraught with biases. For example, research on the family neglected to understand the roles women play as spouse, parent, home-maker, worker, etc., as socially constructed by patriarchy as well as class position. For years, the conceptual model that dominated research assumption was based on Parson's and Bales's dichotomous familial roles: Men filled instrumental needs of the family and women the expressive needs.[8] This work, grounded in the unexamined acceptance of sex roles as prescribed by a socially constructed biological explanation of gender differences, has been a power in shaping the discipline. The result reinforced a picture of a nuclear family that actually existed for only a small percentage of U.S. families. Working-class women, single women, women of color, and lesbian women were denied reality within this model. As West and Zimmerman so effectively argued, even the category once known as "sex" is problematic.[9] The assumed biological dichotomous nature of this category has been called into question, thus making the results of much previous research invalid or at least incom-plete.[10] Problematizing the category of "sex" and using the term "gender," which is conceptualized as socially constructed as well as having biological and psychological aspects, also exposes the heterosexist bias of most sex/gender research and findings. Lesbian and gay research as well as feminist work in sociology has deepened our understanding of sex and gender and its social creation.[11]

The Search for a Feminist Methodology

Feminist criticism of this kind of "methodological sloppiness"[12] challenged the discipline, and the American Sociological Association published guidelines on *The Treatment of Gender in Research* (1985). This is an extremely useful guide for doing research, especially quantitative research. It includes steps to promote gender-bias–free research designs and analyses; it cautions researchers against interpretations of correlations as gender differences when in reality they may be consequences of other factors, such as occupational types, different kinds of tasks, class location, and so on. Most importantly, it stresses the diversity of women's experiences and recommends assessing "gender-related findings from a variety of different perspectives (e.g., sociocultural, historical, structural, biological)" (p. vi). I would add that psychological aspects also be taken into account.

Feminist critique has included a search for something called a feminist methodology. Feminist sociologists have used some of the alternative approaches that already exist in sociology, such as symbolic interactionism and ethnomethodology. Many have found them to be more compatible for understanding women's lives because these methods, often done on the microlevel or at least starting there, incorporate the social context of people's everyday lives. In feminist terms: The microlevel of analysis often helps us to see the personal as the political. There is also an attempt to look for a method that would "incorporate a critique of social science which includes reflections on the sources and potentials of possible knowledge."[13] Women's everyday lives, especially as constituted in the past, have been experienced differently from men's and therefore may produce different knowledge and social understandings.[14] Whether one uses quantitative or qualitative methods, women's lives become the focal point.

Since feminist sociologists have called into question the "male" model of research and the conclusions or the lack of conclusions about women's lives, they have embarked on new studies trying new methods of research or adapting old ones. Some adaptations have led to significant contributions in sociological methods. West and Zimmerman's use of ethnomethodology and Garfinkel's story of Agnes, a male who successfully managed her change of sexual/gender identity,[15] is a major contribution in understanding gender roles that could link the macro/micro aspects of sociological theory and research.[16] West and Zimmerman have deepened our awareness of the importance and complexity of gender identity and the inadequacy of previous research that used sex as an unexamined category of a dichotomous, mutually exclusive variable.

Intensive, focused interviews, a qualitative method with a long tradition in the social sciences, have been particularly helpful in understanding the social context of women's lives and how they intersect with the larger social structures.[17] Interviews that are conducted as mutually constructed conversations between the interviewer and interviewee can lessen the objectification of women (as well as other "subjects") thereby increasing an understanding of how people view themselves in their own context.[18] As Smith stated: "Taking the standpoint of women means recognizing that as inquirers we are brought into determinate relations with those whose experience we intend to express."[19]

However, as promising as this methodology may be, it can lend itself to inaccurate generalization when too much similarity of relationship between the interviewer and the interviewed is assumed. Catherine Riessman analyzed the form and content of two interviews done by a white interviewer, one with an Anglo woman and one with a Puerto Rican woman, to show that the assumption of shared gender identity is insufficient to fully understand the discourse and narrative of the Puerto Rican woman's story. Class, ethnicity, and cultural dimensions also shape our social context and our concomitant expression of it to others as well as to ourselves. Women's lives are not simply determined by our gender identity.

The envoicement of the complexity, diversity, and ultimately the richness of textured lives can be missed by interviewers who do not understand allusions and nuances of a life with which they are not familiar. Riessman summed up the discussion on the methodological tensions for sociologists when she concluded her article by stating that: "good life history interviewing requires attending to the voice of the life world . . . and a corresponding muting of the voice of science . . . letting our subjects' voices speak for themselves. . . . As social scientists, we do not relive experiences but interpret and generalize. However, if a sensitive collaboration has not occurred in the interview and the analysis, we may have 'heard' nothing."[20]

Thus, as with the larger feminist movement, a universalization of white women's lives found its way into our own research, limiting our search. Adding and problematizing gender as a category and including women's experience usually translated into "falsely universalizing the category of 'woman.' Too often the experience of white, middle-class, heterosexual, Euro-American women has served as a basis for analyses that seek to generalize about the experience of WOMAN. The inclusive knowledge we seek should as equally attend to race, class and sexuality as to gender."[21]

Gender as an Interactive Variable

In the section that follows, Cheryl Gilkes joins other feminist sociologists[22] in criticizing this universalization of women's experience and offers a corrective through her own work on, about, and by women of color. Using the basic tenet of feminist research that asserts the need for examining the contexualized lives of women,[23] Gilkes goes to the heart of black women's lives—the community. Previous sociological methods have categorized the variables of race, class, and gender as if they have no relation to each other. By historicizing and contextualizing the community experience of black women, Gilkes has created a multidimensional approach that not only brings to light the interconnectedness of race, class, and gender which operate as a triple oppression but also illuminates the survival strategies of women of color that have enabled them to continue as a viable community. Borrowing Alice Walker's term, Gilkes notes that women of color have begun to conceptualize a "womanist sociology" that "contains a sociology of African American knowledge that implies that personal meeting, spirituality, and moral order within the community are centered in women's wisdom." (See the following section.)

An inclusive model being fashioned by feminists may transform sociology and its methods even further than we have done so far. Understanding the communal strategies of survival and bonding that women have struggled to build and maintain over time may point the way to greater knowledge of who we are in the larger social community and how we are changing our collective consciousness to include difference and diversity as well as commonalities of experience. This new consciousness may be the "crucial corrective" that revolutionizes not only sociology but all the disciplines.

Notes

1. J. Stacey and B. Thorne, "The Missing Feminist Revolution in Sociology," *Social Problems* 32(1985):310–316; D. Smith, *The Everyday World As Problematic: A Feminist Sociology* (Toronto: University of Toronto Press, 1987).

2. C. W. Mills, *The Sociological Imagination* (New York: Oxford University Press, 1959).

3. H. Garfinkel, *Studies in Ethnomethodology* (Cambridge: Polity Press, 1984).

4. M. Horkheimer and T. Adorno, *Dialectic of Enlightenment* (New York: Continuum, 1987); H. Marcuse, *One Dimensional Man* (Boston: Beacon Press, 1966).

5. M. Foucault, *The Archaeology of Knowledge and the Discourse on Language* (New York: Pantheon, 1972); M. Foucault, *The Order of Things: An Archaeology of the Human Sciences* (New York: Vintage Books, 1973).

6. S. Harding, ed., *Feminism and Methodology* (Bloomington: Indiana University Press, 1987).

7. Stacey and Thorne, "The Missing Feminist Revolution."

8. Ibid.

9. C. West and D. Zimmerman, "Doing Gender," *Gender and Society* 1(1987):125–151.

10. A. Fausto-Sterling, *Myths of Gender: Biological Theories About Women and Men* (New York: Basic Books, 1985).

11. C. Kitzinger, *The Social Construction of Lesbianism* (Newbury Park, CA: Sage Publications, 1987).

12. Stacey and Thorne, "The Missing Feminist Revolution."

13. J. Cook and M. M. Fonow, "Knowledge and Women's Interests: Issues of Epistemology and Methodology in Feminist Sociological Research," *Sociological Inquiry* 56(1986):2–29.

14. Smith, *The Everyday World As Problematic*, especially chapters 2 and 3.

15. H. Garfinkel, *Studies in Ethnomethodology*.

16. West and Zimmerman, "Doing Gender," pp. 125–151.

17. D. Segura, "Chicana and Mexican Immigrant Women at Work: The Impact of Class, Race, and Gender on Occupational Mobility," *Gender and Society* 3(1989):37–52.

18. E. G. Mishler, *Research Interviewing: Context and Narrative* (Cambridge: Harvard University Press, 1986).

19. Smith, *The Everyday World As Problematic*.

20. C. K. Riessman, "When Gender is Not Enough," *Gender and Society* 1(1987):172–207.

21. Stacey and Thorne, "The Missing Feminist Revolution," pp. 310–316.

22. B. Omolade, "Black Women and Feminism," in *The Future of Difference*, ed. H. Eisenstein and A. Jardine (New Brunswick, NJ: Rutgers University Press, 1980); C. K. Riessman, "When Gender is Not Enough"; K. Dugger, "Social Location and Gender-Role Attitudes: A Comparison of Black and White Women," *Gender and Society* 2(1988):425–448; L. W. Cannon, E. Higginbotham, and M. L. A. Leung, "Race and Class Bias in Qualitative Research," *Gender and Society* 2(1988):449–462; Segura, "Chicana and Mexican Immigrant Women at Work," 37–52.

23. M. B. Parlee, "Psychology and Women," *Signs* 5(1979):121–133.

A CASE STUDY: RACE-ETHNICITY, CLASS, AND AFRICAN AMERICAN WOMEN: EXPLORING THE COMMUNITY CONNECTION
Cheryl Townsend Gilkes

Many discussions of the African American experience raise the question: "Is it race or is it class?" The very question misdirects the path of inquiry. Race and class always intersect. The problems inherent in attempts to treat them as distinct and unrelated factors are compounded by a confusion between class and status and an attendant failure to account for the historical role of middle classes and their members.[1] Although there is growing recognition and attention to the complexity of these issues, sociological inquiry has not adopted a language or a perspective adequate to explain fully the position and the experiences of peoples of color in the United States. These problems with prevailing perspectives on social class in the United States become exacerbated when the discussion turns to the African American community.[2]

The term race-ethnicity may more accurately direct inquiry. Some scholars have found that the term race-ethnicity grasped the colonial dimensions of racial oppression without negating the particular ethnic experiences and communities of very diverse peoples of color in the United States.[3] The term is an important reminder of the ethnic dimensions of the black experience and it counters those who discount the cultural traditions of black people as simply and only a product of racial oppression.

As members of a racial-ethnic group whose color and historical role in the labor force combined to intensify the experience of oppression, African American women, particularly, have defied analysis from the eurocentric and androcentric perspectives of those who would treat race, class, and gender as discrete and independent entities. Recent attempts by feminist scholars have also fallen short of grasping fully the theoretical dimensions of African American women's experience. Although stunning in their labor and scope, these works are incomplete. Jacqueline Jones's work is the most comprehensive.[4] Her framework is "women's history," and in building that framework, she castigated black women for their commitment to racial solidarity. In her attempt to integrate the experiences of black and white women across racial lines, Jones almost discounted the importance of the ethnic or community dimensions of experience.

Her failure to grasp the centrality of church work and community work, even for the poorest working women, led her to imply that black women's commitments to their community organizations and their churches was a source of their white mistresses' oppression. Describing the problems of white mistresses during the post–Civil War era "in a patriarchal world," she wrote:

> Domestics arrived at work late, left early in the afternoon, or stayed away for days at a time to mark special events and holidays. Communal celebrations in their own neighborhoods took precedence over the needs and expectations of their employers. Revivals periodically inspired sinners to "get religion" and join with others in an ecstasy of newfound salvation. . . . "Excursions"— the chartering of a train for pleasure and fund raising on behalf of a church or benevolent society—proved to be the bane of many a mistress's existence.[5]

Although Jones acknowledged the failure of white power to address the political and economic concerns of black people, at the end of the book she complained:

> Black women's relation to the gender gap remains problematic, for they show little willingness to embrace political candidates endorsed by mainstream white feminist organizations . . . if a black candidate of either sex presents a viable alternative. . . . [B]lack working women tend to filter their political activity through the lenses of black loyalty, a reflection of both the historic and unique impact of racial prejudice on their lives and on the lives of their foremothers. . . .[6]

Similar failures can be found in analyses of the civil rights movement that ignore the roles played by women in leadership, organizational integrity, political education, and mobilization. Only recently has there been work available that grapples adequately with the centrality of black women to this movement.[7] In actuality, in order to comprehend the black female experience, one must understand and explore the "community connection." It is black women's relationship with their entire community—both in consciousness and in practice—that facilitates a unique intersection of race-ethnicity and class as a motive force for social change. Indeed, failure to account for the role of black women in their communities has flawed most analyses of social change and the black experience.

This chapter, then, attempts to account for and interpret the interaction among black women across class lines and to account for what seems to be a unique effort to share consciousness and community across the barriers of social class. It is an interpretation of African American women's history and experience based on data collected on women who achieved prominence as advocates and activists in an urban African American community;[8] additional observations are taken from field work and interviews for a current project on African American churches.[9] Consistent with their historical antecedents in church and politics, black women have been a force for social change through a tradition of activism or "womanist insurgence." This activism has been tied to black women's discovery that communal or group responses to common problems have facilitated women's survival and women's contributions to overall community survival. Such collectivism and traditions of activism have led to the integration of female political leadership across class boundaries and, more recently, has enabled the emergence of a distinct, politically conscious occupational mobility[10] in those helping professions that most directly address the problems faced in urban black communities.

Womanist Insurgence:
The Community Connection

Black women have had a distinctive experience, and their response to that experience has been as distinctive. Some of that distinction has been captured by Alice Walker in her introduction and definition of the term "womanist."[11] Although not a systematic sociological concept or theory, Walker suggested certain directions for anyone seeking to interpret African American women's experience from a point of view that is grounded in the black experience or is africentric in its approach while at the same time acknowledging the importance of the critique of culture stemming from women's experience, generally known as feminist. Walker implied that the womanist approach incorporates a broader and more radical critical scope. First of all, her definition grasps some key historical realities that have emerged as models in the consciousness of black women. Regardless of their social class, many black women are able to name a number of black women, such as Sojourner Truth, Harriet Tubman, Mary Church Terrell, Nannie Helen Burroughs, and Rosa Parks, as role models. Activities in their churches involving both middle-class and working-class women provide opportunities for public "remembering" of these heroines' bold behavior. Walker, as part of her definition, alluded to the boldness of these ancestors, stating, "Traditionally capable, as in: 'Mama, I'm walking to Canada and I'm taking you and a bunch of other slaves with me.' Reply: 'It wouldn't be the first time.' "[12] Obviously, Walker is alluding to Harriet Tubman whose heroic activities as a conductor on the Underground Railway and as a scout for the Union Army are legendary. Both Joyce Ladner and Bonnie Thornton Dill pointed to the importance of strength, self-reliance, and autonomy as elements in a role model that black women view as normative.[13] Ladner's work is crucial because that model is incorporated into the world view of lower-class black girls as well as working women. Dill's observations point to the way in which such a role model contradicts and contrasts with what has been considered normative for white women.

Walker's definition of womanist also contains an incipient sociology of African American knowledge that implies that personal meaning, spirituality, and moral order within the community are centered in women's wisdom. Harking back to Mary Church Terrell's insistence that the black community should be called "colored" because of its high degree of diversity, Walker described a womanist as "Traditionally universalist, as in: 'Mama, why are we brown, pink, and yellow, and our cousins are white, beige, and black?' Ans: 'Well, you know the colored race is just like a flower garden, with every color flower represented.'" For Walker, a womanist is also "[c]ommitted to survival and wholeness of entire people, male *and* female. Not a separatist. . . ."[14] This definition summarizes a diverse historical role played by black women. Historically, women have taken major responsibility for the integrity of the community and for its mobilization.[15]

From a sociological and theoretical perspective, Deborah King addressed the importance of black women's consciousness regarding the entire community. King offered an "interactive model" to account for the "evidence that the importance of the multiple discriminations of race, gender, and class is varied and complex" and to establish that "the relative significance of race, sex, or class in determining the conditions of black women's lives is neither fixed nor absolute but rather dependent on the socio-historical context and the social phenomenon under consideration."[16] Thus the interactions among gender, race-ethnicity, and class in black women's lives "produce what to some appears a seemingly confounding set of social roles and political attitudes among black women." King introduced the terms "multiple jeopardy" and "multiple consciousness" to depict the black women's social reality and their ideological and practical responses. She wrote:

> A black feminist ideology . . . declares the visibility of black women. [It] . . . asserts self-determination as essential. . . . [A] black feminist ideology fundamentally challenges the interstructure of the oppressions of racism, sexism, and classism both in the dominant society and within movements for liberation. It is in confrontation with multiple jeopardy that black women define and sustain a multiple consciousness essential for our liberation.[17]

Anna Julia Cooper (1892) and W.E.B. DuBois (1924), early analysts of the African American experience, pointed out the importance of black people to the political and cultural life of the United States. One of the most important contributions was the persistent challenge to oppression that came from the black community. This challenge, considered a "gift of black folk" by DuBois,[18] forced the extension of the Constitution beyond its originally intended population and "reconstructed democracy" in the South. For Cooper, the conflicts generated by black people were important to forging what she called a "progressive peace," or a more inclusive social order as the result of conflict.[19] It was W.E.B. DuBois who, in his sociology of the United States, argued that America faced "three great revolutions." These were the freeing of labor, the freeing of black people, and the freeing of women; in other words, political and social change that simultaneously addressed class, race-ethnicity, and gender oppression. He saw in black women the intersections of these three great revolutions. Their value to the transformation of this society into the democracy he believed that the United States was in the process of becoming was therefore inestimable.

Additional observations led DuBois to argue that black women should have the vote because they would use it more prudently and in proportionately greater numbers than black men. Calling them "unselfish intelligent voters," DuBois stated flatly that "you cannot bribe Negro women."[20] In assessing the contributions of the black women's club movement, a movement through which black women emerged in the first decades of the twentieth century as "the intellectual leadership of the Race," DuBois noted that "the women of America who are doing humble but on the whole the most effective work in the social uplift of the lowly, *not so much by money* as by personal contact, are the colored women."[21] DuBois's emphasis on their lack of money indicates that the movement, fueled by the motto "Lifting as we climb," involved women of all social classes.

Anna Julia Cooper also recognized the critical importance of black women to their race and to the society at large; her perspective is embodied in the now-famous quotation, "Only the BLACK WOMAN can say 'when and where I enter, in the quiet, undisputed dignity of my womanhood, without violence and without suing or special patronage, then and there the whole *Negro race enters with me.'*"[22] Both DuBois and Cooper saw the full emancipation of black women as a key to America's greatness and as the nexus of a struggle involving the intersection of class and labor status, ethnic experience, and the special perspective of the femininity that had transcended the harem-like demands of the dominant culture. According to Cooper, "the colored woman of today occupies, one may say, a unique position in this country. . . . She is confronted by both a woman question and a race problem and is as yet an unknown or an unacknowledged factor in both."[23]

Black women, then, had to be comprehended as a unique social entity and as the key to democratic progress and moral order. Their situation combined issues and experiences that presented a peculiar challenge to the society and to all other social movements.

Black women's own consciousness about the intersection of work (and therefore class), race-ethnicity, and gender in their experience led to political activism that was self-consciously female. The black women's club movement consciously reached across social classes to forge networks among women "in professions" and "in industry." The movement was also avidly antiseparatist. One key leader, Josephine St. Pierre Ruffin, invited men to join the movement and, therefore, to follow women leaders. Womanist insurgence, then, insisted upon leading men in a patriarchal society by means of autonomous women's organizations that were open to men. Their leaders made it clear that they were "neither alienating nor withdrawing," but simply "coming to the front" seeking to offer leadership.

The current political sophistication of these women, across class lines, is the product of the "personal contact" that was part and parcel of their club movement. One woman I interviewed described the way in which one of the clubs she founded dealt solely with the problems of black women who were household domestics, teaching them to carry their carfare to their daywork jobs and to "leave the money on the table" when employers sought to cheat them out of promised wages. Although her husband was a white-collar technician who manufactured appliances for doctors, she worked as a household domestic before and after marriage and therefore felt moved to reach out to "other women like myself." She noted that the clubs were training stations for black women leaders who learned the language and the politics that enabled them to lead clubs and become public women. Black church women similarly sought to develop grassroots leadership by training southern urban and rural women to be public speakers at the turn of the century. A notable example is found in Nannie Helen Burroughs's rationale for the instituting of "Women's Day" in black Baptist churches in 1907, a practice that spread to every predominantly black church denomination and to "black congregations within predominantly white denominations such as the United Methodist Church, the United Church of Christ, the United Presbyterian Church, and the Disciples of Christ-Christian."[24] According to Burroughs it was a day "primarily for raising women" and "a glorious opportunity for women to learn to speak for themselves. . . ."[25] Womanist insurgence, activism rooted in the multiple consciousness Deborah King[26] attributed to black women, entailed an individual and collective autonomy "in thousands of churches and social clubs, in missionary societies and fraternal organizations, in unions like the

National Association of Colored Women . . . ministering to all sorts of needs."[27]

Historical Discovery:
Strength in Community

Such efforts fostered and continued a collective ethic among black women that had its roots in slavery. Only in the past two decades have we learned much about the communal lives of enslaved black people with the emergence of a dynamic social history focused on the slave community.[28] The roots of the black religious experience with its invisible church and formally organized churches[29] and of the family with its emphasis on commitments to extended kin[30] were developed during this period. These two institutions, we now know, contributed mightily to the physical and psychic survival of black people during slavery. This revisionist history of slavery is important because it provides an opportunity to examine the human response to slavery both as an inhumane economic institution and as a crucible for human community.

Several scholars have pointed to the importance and durability of the family.[31] Although the administration of family life by slave owners was intrusive and arbitrary, family commitments were deep and durable with voluntary family disruption minimal.[32] Slave mothers took seriously the role of their husbands, and Gutman[33] points to the importance of naming systems, which indicated the importance of fathers and husbands to black people even though slave owners did not think them important enough to record. The high rate of mother-headed families in the urban experience should not be read backwards into slavery.[34] The family was also an important agency of socialization to a clearly articulated set of norms and values that enabled black people to survive and to cope. Women were prominent as principals in this process. Women's roles in religious and cultural socialization led to their participation as leaders for the entire community.[35]

Black people not only built a family tradition but also a religious tradition. The church was an important broker in enabling black people to resolve the pain and stress of death and disruption. The "invisible institution" was open to the participation of women as religious leaders. Toni Morrison, in her recent book *Beloved*,[36] built on this tradition in her characterization of "Baby Suggs holy"—inspired by Margaret Garner's mother-in-law, an antebellum preacher or "professor of religion."[37] According to other historians, black women played prominent roles in the organizational establishment and cultural maintenance of churches.[38] Men who left their autobiographies in the slave narratives attributed their early spirituality to the religious practice, especially prayer traditions, of their mothers and aunts, the women of their slave communities.[39]

The participation of black women in establishing the family and the church during slavery does not explain fully the collective ethos that binds black women across social class. Although their contribution to these institutions was and is considerable, another dimension of the black female experience must be taken into account. Deborah Gray White, the only historian to focus exclusively on black women's experience during slavery, has not only pointed to the centrality of women to the family and the religious experience but also described and analyzed the life that black women shared with each other.[40] It is my conclusion that the "female slave network" White described was a third institution that, together with the institutions of church and of family, fostered the physical and psychic survival of black people during slavery.

White argued that the image of black women as strong is an accurate one, but that that strength did not simply appear. "Strength had to be cultivated. It came no more naturally to [black women] than to anyone, slave or free, male or female, black or white. If they seemed exceptionally strong it was partly because they often functioned in groups and derived strength from numbers."[41] In addition to the work that they accomplished with men and sometimes like men, White showed that slave women spent most of their time with each other. They depended upon each other for medical care and child care. Within their network, these women created and maintained a pecking order based largely on age and occupation. Their leadership sometimes extended beyond the bounds of the women's network and could disrupt plantation operations. Some women emerged as spiritual leaders, and slave women had a tradition of autonomous rituals and prayer meetings.

The female slave network was necessary for the survival of slave women and their families. By extension, then, it was a necessary feature of life within the entire slave community. According to White:

> The supportive atmosphere of the female community was buffer enough against the depersonalizing regime of plantation work and the general dehumanizing nature of slavery. When we consider how much more confined to the plantation women were than men, that many women had husbands who visited only once or twice a week, and that on average slave women outlived slave men by two years, we realize just how important the female community was to its members.[42]

Black women continued to assume public roles within their community after emancipation. Their commitment to that community was intensified through the female network and that female community continues to exert an important historical force to this day. As White observed: "[S]lave women had ample opportunity to develop a consciousness grounded in their identity as females. . . . [A]dult female cooperation and interdependence was a fact of female slave life. The self-reliance and self-sufficiency of slave women, therefore, must not only be viewed in the context of what the individual slave woman did for herself, but what slave women as a group were able to do for one another."[43] It is such a consciousness that survived and was sustained in facing the problems of reconstruction and its aftermath. According to White, evidence of this strength in collectivism was found in the Sea Islands and other areas of the South.[44] The complex and concentrated character of black women's oppression formed the practical basis for such cooperation and bonding. White concluded: "Few women who knew the pain of childbirth or who understood the agony and depression that flowed from sexual harrassment and exploitation survived without friends, without female company. . . . Treated by Southern whites as if they were anything but self-respecting females, [they] could forge their own independent definition of woman-hood through the female network. . . ."[45]

The continuing force of this third institution comes through in the political and community history of black women. Echoes of this network are found in DuBois's observation that "personal contact" rather than money was the principal resource through which black women did their work for social uplift. The continuing force of this network can also be found in the women's organizations of churches and the widespread popularity of "Women's Day" in nearly all black churches—a day in which black women's own "independent definition of womanhood" is ritually enforced.[46] Over a period of forty years, 1895 to 1935, black women managed to bring together a massive network of women's organizations that were able to mobilize leadership at national and local levels. Paula Giddings pointed to the emergence of national leaders such as Mary McLeod Bethune as examples of this mobilization.[47] The effectiveness of their organizations was such that Betty Friedan, speaking to the Eastern Sociological Society in 1974, pronounced black women "already organized."

This collectivism and community integration among women accounts for the very different orientation of black and white feminists. Gloria Watkins, describing her first encounter with women's studies at Stanford University, observed, "white women were reveling in the joy of being together—to them it was an important, momentous occasion."[48] Reflecting on her own life among "black Americans living in a small Kentucky town" she described a life style that contradicted that of her fellow students. She wrote, "I had not known a life where women had not been together, where women had not helped, protected, and loved one another deeply." Watkins is acknowledging what other analysts have observed, that there is a collective ethos among black women within black communities.[49] The term "sisterhood," for white women a goal of the feminist movement, is a reality and part of the larger black "familyhood" in settings such as churches, community organizations, and fraternal orders where "mother," "father," "brother," and "sister" are the terms of address and family is the metaphor for community.

Community, Class, and the Integration of Female Leadership

The diverse problems faced by black communities generate leadership from all social levels. Though one would expect that class origins would be a barrier, there are specific contexts that historically have integrated black women, sometimes consciously, across the possible barriers of social class. Indeed, more than any other ethnic group, black people have wrestled with class as an ideology and a social problem. Not only have there been publications that have criticized the role, behavior, and values of elites, E. Franklin Frazier's *Black Bourgeoisie*[50] to name only one, but there also has been a strong public critique of class as a reality that divides the community, especially in churches and political organizations.

As we have seen, the two contexts that have integrated black women have been the church and autonomous women's organizations. Because most sociological and historical analyses of religion examine the role of male leaders or congregational culture, we have little understanding of the role of black women in national religious networks from a perspective of institutional history.[51] One study, still in progress, argues that the negative impact of recent social changes affecting opportunities for black men (negative in their potential for siphoning off talented male leadership from the religious communities) has been blunted by the emergence of black women in the ministry. However, the recent movement of women into the more visible clergy positions is part of a larger history in which the very integrity of religious organizations has been tied to the enterprise of women. As the chief economic investors in religious organizations, black women found ways, collective and powerful ways, to exercise influence in spite of discrimination.[52] It has been through the church that poor women have had access to affluent women and that affluent women have maintained their commitments to poor women, regardless of other socially exclusive activities in which they may have participated. An important part of religious history has been the insistence on a model of women's leadership that stands with the masses and not above.[53]

The other context for the integration of black women across class lines has been autonomous women's organizations—the organizations that reflect Walker's definition of the womanist approach to women's politics, "Not separatist, except periodically, for health."[54] The emergence of the black women's club movement coincided with the very sexist assault on female leadership within black churches and what Evelyn Brooks Barnett described as black Baptist women's loss of the battle over the pulpit. Not only did church women use their women's clubs to carry on leadership roles outside the confines of their churches, but they also formed autonomous and highly elaborate women's organizations within their churches. For these women, the development of acculturated grassroots leadership was a principle task. The club movement sent organizers into the rural South, particularly in states that were not represented at the national meetings of the National Association of Colored Women. Nannie Helen Burroughs, as the principal proponent of a national women's day in National Baptist Convention churches, provided speeches for women from the national office in order to foster the development of public speakers in local congregations—so women could learn to speak up for themselves.[55] Evidence from both fieldwork and historical sources indicates that a real motive of educated women in movement and church clubs was grassroots socialization and leadership development. Their Christian ideology made them insist upon outreach to foster a genuine equality among black women.

In the late nineteenth and the first half of the twentieth century (1895–1965), the shared experiences of racism in the labor force provided an additional context of shared consciousness. Women interviewed in my own study and in the Black Women's Oral History Project described their activities working with household domestics. Queen Mother Moore, a former Garveyite, described her own privileged upbringing in Louisiana and her early campaign to challenge the consciousness of other privileged black people. Born to a Louisiana Creole family, she described an incident where, at the age of five, she "ordered" her "nurse" to return home and get her a new handkerchief. She told me, "I was raised to be a real bourgeois 'stinker.'" Later she was instrumental in forming the movement that influenced Mayor LaGuardia to remove the "slave markets"—places where black women waited for opportunities for day work. Another woman, director of an organization that lobbied for legislation protecting domestics, described her sense of commitment, reminding me that her mother along with most other black working women had performed household service in order to enable her family and the community organizations she supported to survive. A number of the clubs affiliated with the National Association of Colored Women sought to provide women "in industry" with alternative cultural experiences that would be emotionally uplifting and to counter the effects of demeaning work. One working-class churchwoman described the "beautiful cultural events" she attended regularly at a local club house. Another elderly clubwoman described the practice of *not* asking "What do you do?" in order to emphasize the importance placed upon getting to know the person at social gatherings rather than getting to know her occupational status.

Both club and church reinforced the consciousness of a shared racial oppression. Historically, as class differentiation became more evident, women in both settings actively countered the growing divisions among themselves. Although class and color are significant forces in marriage markets and socializing, many black women whose privileges could easily distance them from the grassroots, participate in church and community organizations that focus directly and indirectly on the shared suffering of black women. In those community contexts that directly challenge the dominant culture or foster material and psychic survival, conscious integration of women across class continues to be a significant manifestation of black women's strength through collectivism.

Racism and Womanist Consciousness

It is no accident that racism is named in the events giving rise to autonomous black women's movements while sexism, until very recently and still ambivalently, is not named in black women's responses to patriarchal black institutions such as the church. Historically, evidence of racism has been the galvanizing force. In the late nineteenth century, the insults heaped upon Ida B. Wells and other black women as they sought to end lynching helped to mobilize church and professional women nationally. Newspaper editors, seeking to discredit black women activists, such as Ida B. Wells, levelled accusations at them and black women in general.[56] Later, the women's suffrage movement appealed to the racism in the South for votes for women, while barring the participation of black women in the white suffrage movement.[57] In contemporary times, responses to the Moynihan report and its attack on the work and family roles of black women sparked a contemporary activism around the problems of black women.[58] Stereotypes of black women, usually some variation of the "Mammy" and "Jezebel," then and now, revolve around their work and family roles. Racist assaults typically intersect race with labor status and sexual status and manage to pervade the meaning system of the wider culture.

In one of the most dramatic examples of the pervasive cultural image of black women, Audre Lorde described her experience in a supermarket: "I wheel my two-year-old daughter in a shopping cart through a supermarket in Eastchester in 1967, and a little white girl riding past in her mother's cart calls out excitedly, 'Oh look, Mommy, a baby maid!'" Lorde then pointed out that such a stereotype is reinforced in the reaction of the white mother. She added, "And your mother shushes you, but she does not correct you." Because of that failure to correct, the barrier of racism within the feminist movement is firmly in place; Lorde observed, "And fifteen years later, at a [feminist] conference on racism, you can still find that story humorous. But I hear your laughter is full of terror and dis-ease."[59]

What Lorde described, a microcosm of so many of the culturally pervasive stereotypes of black women, is a fusion of work and its meaning (labor status), color, and gender that sees black women, regardless of age and social class, as perpetual characters on the stage of demeaning and degrading work. The cultural configuration is so formalized that young children have internalized these images of a permanent servant class. Many black women recognize that middle-class managerial roles do not negate this image.[60] One woman I interviewed, a former college dean, described her humiliation at a university convocation reception when a new, white woman faculty member approached her to ask for help in securing a domestic servant. Such incidents reinforced her determination to continue to live in "the ghetto" in order to be the kind of role model that others had been when she had been a member of the underclass. This sense of shared humiliation and the determination to resist its consequences have undergirded the community experience of black women and helped to define the character of their relationships with one another.

The community activities of black women and the political and cultural histories tied to these activities are the observable consequences of a distinctive multiple consciousness that transcends the boundaries of class. The shared problems stemming from racism moved women to organize consciously across class lines and consequently to discover the diverse dimensions of the economic and political problems faced by black communities. While sociological analysis still puzzles over the question of race *or* class, more recent approaches, particularly the work of King and Collins,[61] address their interactive and interstructured reality in the lives of African American women. Understanding the community connection among women and between women and men provides an important perspective on the way womanist practices and insurgence have incorporated the many particularities of history through a conscious class integration in the context of community and church work.

Notes

1. R. Vanneman and L. W. Cannon, *The American Perception of Class* (Philadelphia: Temple University Press, 1987).

2. E. Higginbotham, "Just Who Is Black and Middle Class?" (Toronto, Canada: Paper presented to the Society for the Study of Social Problems); B. Landry, *The New Black Middle Class* (Los Angeles: University of California Press, 1987).

3. B. T. Dill, "Race, Class, and Gender: Prospects for an All-Inclusive Sisterhood," *Feminist Studies* 9(1983):131–150.

4. J. Jones, *Labor of Love, Labor of Sorrow: Black Women, Work and Family from Slavery to the Present* (New York: Basic Books, 1985).

5. Ibid., p. 133.

6. Ibid., pp. 328–329.

7. S. Clark, *Ready from Within: Septima Clark and the Civil Rights Movement* (Navarro, CA: Wild Trees Press, 1986); P. Giddings, *When and Where I Enter: The Impact of Black Women on Race and Sex in America* (New York: William Morrow and Company, 1984); M. King, *Freedom Song: A Personal Story of the 1960s Civil Rights Movement* (New York: William Morrow and Company, 1987); A. Morris, *The Origins of the Civil Rights Movement: Black Communities Organizing for Change* (New York: Free Press, 1984); J.A.G. Robinson, *The Montgomery Bus Boycott and the Women Who Started It* (Knoxville: University of Tennessee Press, 1986).

8. C. T. Gilkes, "Living and Working in a World of Trouble: The Emergent Career of the Black Woman Community Worker" (Boston: Northeastern University, Ph.D. Dissertation, 1979); C. T. Gilkes, "Going Up for the Oppressed: The Career Mobility of Black Women Community Workers," *Journal of Social Issues* 39(1983):115–139.

9. C. T. Gilkes, "Together and in Harness: Women's Traditions in the Sanctified Church," *Signs* 10(1985):678–699; C. T. Gilkes, "The Role of Women in the Sanctified Church," *Journal of Religious Thought* 43(1986):24–41.

10. Gilkes, "Going Up for the Oppressed."

11. A. Walker, *In Search of Our Mothers' Gardens: Womanist Prose* (New York: Harcourt, Brace, Jovanovich, 1983).

12. Ibid., p. xi.

13. J. Ladner, *Tomorrow's Tomorrow* (Garden City, NY: Doubleday and Company, 1971).

14. Walker, *In Search of Our Mothers' Gardens*, p. xi.

15. Robinson, *The Montgomery Bus Boycott*.

16. D. K. King, "Multiple Jeopardy, Multiple Consciousness: The Context of a Black Feminist Ideology," *Signs* 14(1988):42–72.

17. Ibid., p. 72.

18. W.E.B. DuBois, *The Gift of Black Folk: The Negroes in the Making of America* (New York: Washington Square Press, 1924, 1970), pp. 65–140.

19. A. J. Cooper, *A Voice from the South by a Woman of the South* (New York: Negro Universities Press, 1969; Ohio: Aldine Publishing House, 1892), p. 151.

20. W.E.B. DuBois, *W.E.B. DuBois: The Crisis Writings*, ed. Daniel Walden (Greenwich, CT: Fawcett Publications, Inc., 1972), p. 351.

21. Ibid., p. 340.

22. Cooper, *A Voice from the South*, p. 31.

23. Ibid., p. 134.

24. J. Dodson and C. T. Gilkes, "Something Within: Social Change and Collective Endurance in the Sacred World of Black Christian Women," in *Women and Religion in America, Volume 3: 1900–1968*, ed. R. R. Ruether and R. S. Keller (San Francisco: Harper and Row Publishers, 1986), pp. 88–89.

25. Ibid., pp. 122, 125.

26. King, "Multiple Jeopardy, Multiple Consciousness."

27. DuBois, *The Gift of Black Folk*, p. 149.

28. J. Blassingame, *The Slave Community: Plantation Slavery in the Antebellum South* (New York: Oxford University Press, 1972); E. Fox-Genovese, *Within the Plantation Household: Black and White Women of the Old South* (Chapel Hill: University of North Carolina Press, 1988); E. Genovese, *Roll, Jordan, Roll: The World the Slaves Made* (New York: Random House, 1975); D. G. White, *Ar'n't I a Woman?: Female Slaves in the Plantation South* (New York: W. W. Norton and Company, 1985).

29. M. Creel, *A Peculiar People: Slave Religion and Community-Culture Among the Gullahs* (New York: New York University Press, 1988); A. J. Raboteau, *Slave Religion: The Peculiar Institution in the Antebellum South* (New York: Oxford University Press, 1978); M. Sobel, *Trabelin' On: The Slave's Journey to an Afro-Baptist Faith* (Westport, CT: Greenwood Press, 1979).

30. H. G. Gutman, *The Black Family in Slavery and Freedom, 1750–1924* (New York: Pantheon Books/Random House, 1976); T. L. Webber, *Deep Like the Rivers: Education in the Slave Quarter Community, 1831–1865* (New York: W. W. Norton and Company, 1978).

31. Genovese, *Roll, Jordan, Roll*; Gutman, *Black Family in Slavery*.

32. Blassingame, *The Slave Community*.

33. Gutman, *Black Family in Slavery*.

34. Dill, "Race, Class, and Gender"; Gutman, *Black Family in Slavery*.

35. Webber, *Deep Like the Rivers*.

36. T. Morrison, *Beloved* (New York: Random House, 1987).

37. M. Harris, M. Levitt, R. Furman, and E. Smith, *The Black Book* (New York: Random House, 1974), p. 10.

38. L. Litwack, *Been in the Storm So Long: The Aftermath of Slavery* (New York: Random House, 1979), pp. 461–462; White, "Ar'n't I a Woman," pp. 137–138.

39. Webber, *Deep Like the Rivers*.

40. White, "Ar'n't I a Woman."

41. Ibid., p. 119.

42. Ibid., pp. 131–132.

43. Ibid., p. 120.

44. Ibid., p. 140.

45. Ibid., p. 141.

46. Dodson and Gilkes, "Something Within."

47. Giddings, *When and Where I Enter.*

48. B. Hooks, *Feminist Theory: From Margin to Center* (Boston: South End Press, 1984), p. 11.

49. Dill, "Race, Class, and Gender"; Ladner, *Tomorrow's Tomorrow.*

50. F. E. Frazier, *The Black Bourgeoisie* (New York: Free Press, 1957).

51. E. B. Barnett, "Nannie Burroughs and the Education of Black Women," in *The Afro-American Woman: Struggles and Images,* ed. S. Harley and R. Terborg-Penn (Port Washington, NY: Kennikat Press, 1978); E. Brooks, "The Feminist Theology of the Black Baptist Church, 1880–1900," in *Class, Race, and the Dynamics of Control,* ed. A. Swerdlow and H. Lessinger (Boston: G. K. Hall, 1983).

52. Gilkes, "Together and in Harness."

53. Dodson and Gilkes, "Something Within," pp. 126–127.

54. Walker, *In Search of Our Mothers' Gardens,* p. xi.

55. Dodson and Gilkes, "Something Within."

56. Giddings, *When and Where I Enter.*

57. B. H. Andolsen, *"Daughters of Jefferson, Daughters of Bootblacks": Racism and American Feminism* (Macon, GA: Mercer University Press, 1986).

58. T. Cade, *The Black Woman: An Anthology* (New York: New American Library, 1970).

59. A. Lorde, *Sister Outsider: Essays and Speeches* (Trumansburg, NY: Crossing Press, 1984), p. 126.

60. R. G. Dumas, "Dilemmas of Black Females in Leadership," in *The Black Woman,* ed. L. Rodgers-Rose (Beverly Hills, CA: Sage Publications, 1980).

61. King, "Multiple Jeopardy, Multiple Consciousness"; P. H. Collins, "Learning from the Outsider Within: The Sociological Significance of Black Feminist Thought," *Social Problem* 33(1986).

5
ANTHROPOLOGY: FEMINIST METHODOLOGIES FOR THE SCIENCE OF MAN?

Rayna Rapp

Anthropologists assign central value to the power of ancestors, so my discussion of recent developments in feminist anthropology begins with an ancestor legend. In the 1920s, while teaching anthropology in London, Bronislaw Malinowski, one of the truly great figures in modern Anglo-American anthropology, was asked for a definition of the field. "It is the science of man," he is alleged to have replied. "And what about woman?" queried a student in the back of the seminar room. "Ah," came Malinowski's response, "It is the science of man embracing woman."

With such origins, how did feminist anthropology emerge in the early 1970s as one of the most audacious sites of feminist thinking in the social sciences? Given what the French would call the "ordinary sexism" constructed at (and constructing) the heart of the field, why were feminist practitioners of anthropology able to mount a sustained critique from within? There are undoubtedly many roots that nourished this recent history. Among them, I would emphasize three: The first is the mobilizing anger that women studying and teaching anthropology felt, once feminism as a political movement became part of American political culture. For with its arrival, they had to confront the trivialization of women as objects of scientific study, as well as their own role as "scientific" observers. The assumption that male informants held all the interesting information in a given society, the analysis of kinship and marriage patterns from the viewpoint of a male ego, the marginalization of much of women's discourse to gossip—the discovery of these social facts was paralleled by an awareness of the institutionalized discrimination practiced against women as researchers and faculty members in the world of scholarship.

A second reason for the development of a feminist anthropology lies in the pressure exerted more directly on the field by political groups outside the academy. Whenever politically active women demanded an explanation of male dominance, orthodox Marxists suggested a reading of Friedrich Engels for the complete explanation of female oppression.[1] What a convenient book! Despite its many merits, its integrationist politics dutifully served the interests of those progressive parties and movements that did not want to change their analyses or strategies to respond to feminist demands. In the same period, many self-taught feminist scholars began to publish research about Early Woman. Like Engels, they looked to a golden age for the female of the species. In the works of Elizabeth Gould Davis, Evelyn Reed, and Helen Diner, compelling, if mythic, visions of female empowerment were constructed.[2] Quite suddenly, the Matriarchy Question, presumed dead and buried in modern anthropology, resurfaced from many locations in political culture, and academic anthropologists felt it necessary to address the question.

A third and salient reason for the rapid development of a feminist anthropology was the existence of available concepts within classic anthropological discourse. Although I might argue that they were incompletely or even badly theorized, a grab bag of concepts was already present in the canons of our scholarship. They were used to describe sexual symbolism, the sexual division of labor, and sexual segregation of activities and values which fieldworkers had noted in a myriad of traditional societies. These provided minimal scaffolding on which to hang our new, naive, and politically energetic questions concerning sexual oppression.

In light of these developments, a generation of newly feminist anthropologists set off to conduct their fieldwork and to recatalogue their library knowledge, armed with a new set of questions. Much of the initial work consisted of testing, rejecting, or refashioning the classic methodologies of the field. In the last fifteen years, we have produced many contentious, woman-centered theories of our own. And in this process, we have learned to examine received methodologies and to name their political implications. To illustrate with some of the most obvious examples:

- Sally Slocum's focus on the division of labor by sex restored female activity to the analysis of human evolution.[3] In creating "Woman the Gatherer" as a challenge to "Man the Hunter," did she also materialize women as "naturally" productive and nurturant?
- Gayle Rubin's romp through the marriage systems constructed by Claude Levi-Strauss led her to sound a utopian call for the abolition

of kinship.[4] Her very influential essay forced us to ask ourselves, "What *is* sex/gender, and can it be freed from the rules of kinship?"

- Michelle Rosaldo's analysis of public/domestic domains as a universal feature of social organization had many implications.[5] One was that women's domestic traditions are worth reevaluation. This perspective directly fed the "difference" debates in international feminist scholarship. Another was that the orthodox Marxist notion of emancipating women by dragging them into social production was insufficient, perhaps irrelevant, unless men were integrated into domestic activities as well. But did such a methodological about-face romanticize an historically specific moment of Western ideology as a universal description of womankind's experiences?

New Methodologies

Feminist anthropologists have also had to invent new methodologies in the narrower sense of the term: We needed new techniques, or toolkits, to get the information we wanted about women. For example, Ximena Bunster and her colleagues undertook an ambitious study of marketing women in Lima, Peru. Their feminist research team was told by other experts that they would never succeed in using a survey instrument to question the women, for they are often recent migrants, usually semi- or nonliterate, inarticulate, and preoccupied with the chores of daily survival. Undaunted, Bunster and her colleagues invented a woman-centered method. They photographed some marketing women at work and at home and requested them to organize the picture into a book. The "talking pictures" functioned as a *fotonovella*, a True Romance comic book story that other women could rapidly read.[6] The team took the book to a wide array of women, who were fascinated to see their lives in this form. Responding to the pictures, they told marvelous, detailed stories about home, love, pregnancy, children, work, politics, and many other salient topics. The "inarticulate" articulate with great clarity, when their own lives are brought into view! Such information is collected by going "where the action isn't," as Beverly Chinas reminded us.[7] It is born in negation. It requires patience, creativity, and a commitment to the importance of female participation, as well as its suppression, as a central research question. At the very least, such information yields a new set of insights into some old questions. At the greatest, it advances an ambitious claim to transform both the questions asked and the field within which they are answered.

To illustrate both those minimalist and maximalist strategies of feminist method, I will briefly discuss three research areas on which

American (and, sometimes, Anglo-American) anthropologists have focussed: the question of human origins; the culturalization of biology and analysis of sex and gender as social constructions; and the critique of universal theory in light of differences among women (that is, the recognition of Others within the Other). Each deserves many books, but here I can only devote a few bibliographic paragraphs to an overview of these important theoretical arenas.

The Question of Human Origins

For North American anthropologists, the question of human origins is a central one. Trained in the neoevolutionist tradition, we place great weight on our origin tales, ordering our beginnings, so that they lead to unified views of our species' progress. Man the Hunter has been challenged by Woman the Gatherer, and the field of physical anthropology is surely being transformed. A group of feminist physical anthropologists and primatologists (Adrienne Zihlman, Nancy Tanner, Jane Lancaster, Phyllis Dolinhow, Thelma Rowell, Frances Burton, and others) joined Sally Slocum in exploring the social implications of maternal-infant bonding; protolanguage acquisition through protokinship; and the relative lateness and minor significance of large-scale game hunting in the evolutionary record.[8] Collectively, these feminist researchers have been enormously creative. They have forced the field to recognize the importance of gathering, of sharing, and of nurturing the young as central aspects of human evolution. From them, we have learned to see that human evolutionary biology always has a social context. Food-sharing and the transmission of culture (itself ultimately dependent on language) are crucial to the female offspring-centered necessities of higher primate and hominid social organization.

Yet, as Donna Haraway tells us, these "Daughters of Man the Hunter" are engaged in contests for meaning amongst themselves.[9] *The Woman Who Never Evolved* and *The Sexual Contract* are in part a response to this view of maternity as central to human evolution in an active, not just a passive, way. And Lucy has also reclaimed some theoretical turf.[10] Fighting with fossils, parrying primates, manipulating monkeys—these are scientific strategies that owe a great deal to the battle of the sexes taking place inside and outside university walls. What is at stake in the struggle over origin tales is our understanding of the importance of the division of labor by sex, the reproductive control (or autonomy) of female primates, and the passivity or activity of females in general. These are surely modern questions whose metaphorical importance lies in present political culture and not simply in the paleolithic.

The Culture of Gender

A second arena in which feminist anthropologists have focussed creative attention has been the radical culturalization of biology. Recent feminist anthropologists remind us that biology is mute; it only speaks to us through cultural translation and is given different voices according to particular social relations. In the West, specific relations condition and create "biology" as a scientific field of investigation. We then draw a picture of "woman" out of scientific (and, increasingly, medicalized) perspectives on female embodiment. But other cultures map women quite differently. Through what Bordieu called "inscriptions in the body," practices as ordinary as female posture and as extraordinary as female genital operations, puberty rites, sexual taboos and possibilities, childbirth, aging, and death itself create the meaning of gender out of embodiment.[11] Women (and men) have what Lucille Newman called "lived bodies," creations of culture, not simply of nature.[12] Using this more phenomenological and cultural-historical perspective, feminist anthropologists have reexamined the female life cycle as it inscribes women. A veritable cottage industry has sprung up to manufacture analyses of pregnancy. The ecology of prenatal practices and birthing, the social construction of motherhood, shifts in birthing practices as they reflect broad social movement, and other power relations of gender and kinship have all been analyzed.[13] Current research on pregnancy in the United States includes a symbolic analysis of the politics of abortion, racial and class differences in young women's discourses on menstruation and pregnancy, and the cultural meaning of high-technological intervention into pregnancy.[14]

Sexuality

Sexuality (not to be conflated with reproduction) has also assumed increasing importance in the work of feminist anthropologists and anthropologically minded historians. Ortner and Whitehead's edited collection, *Sexual Meaning*, contains some excellent analyses of sexual beliefs and practices in non-Western contexts. Especially noteworthy is Whitehead's discussion of the "gender leakage" in institutionalized transvestism among Native American peoples.[15] Blackwood has written an interesting response focussing on the contentious question of cross-cultural lesbianism.[16] Vance is currently exploring the sociomedical and cultural implications of AIDS, and Rubin is analyzing the genesis of gay male urban culture and its social institutions.[17] Such analyses owe a great deal to Foucault's power discourse model, on the one hand, and feminist oral and social history, on the other.[18] Collectively, such disparate studies of sexuality help us to make a simple point once we culturalize, rather than naturalize, women: The social space in which "biological" experiences are constructed is intimately shared with other social relations. Our new focus on sexuality parallels our understandings of other power domains which in many ways invent and constrain both sex and gender. Such a perspective frees us to examine Western culture, as well as the other cultures traditionally subject to anthropological bombardment. And we have come to see the connection of "nature" to "woman" as an historically situated moment in the metaphors of domination that flourish in the West. Such a perspective links feminist anthropologists to their counterparts in literary criticism, critical sociology, and other trends— both social-historical and postmodernist—in intellectual history.

Critique of Universal Theory

Feminist critiques of the history of theory have broken important ground in situating our own position within our analysis. For surely, we must acknowledge that we produce theory predominantly as Western, white, academic feminists, heirs to a tradition of resolutely bourgeois integrationism in the long march of culture. And the Leisure of the Theory Class always runs the risk of false universalization, in this case, granting a unified Woman equal intellectual rights with Man. Yet from the essays in Nature, Culture and Gender, we have come to better understand how the nature/culture opposition flowered from the eighteenth century forward, first as a critique of dominant political philosophies and then as a support of them.[19] From Rosaldo's self-critique on the abuses of feminist anthropology, we see how nineteenth-century sociology created an image of the family as a natural unit embedded in a fiercely competitive marketplace.[20] Feminist theory that uses the public/domestic opposition as a fulcrum owes much to this theoretical moment.[21] When we use the "doubled vision of feminist theory,"[22] we see that the cultural antinomies of production/reproduction, labor/leisure, factory/home, rational/affective personalities as labels for separate spheres assigned to males and females represent one moment in the construction of a single, complex, highly mediated life-way. But these are not immutable, global, or scientific descriptions of a transhistorical reality.[23]

Indeed, that life-way itself is now fragmenting and recomposing, and its cultural categories are being transformed. Donna Haraway's "Manifesto for Cyborgs" reproaches both Marxists and feminists for taking the objects of nineteenth-century classical social theory—production (male) and reproduction (female)—as eternal verities.[24] With the crisis of classic industrial capitalism has come a more multicentric, decentered economy. Transformations of women's experiences through mass education for Western women, increasing paid labor-force participation, decreasing importance of full-time mothering as the normative site of female experience, movements of sexual transformation now beg us to reconceptualize the objects of our theory. If not, we run the risk of romanticizing the very conditions we seek to analyze, inflating them into an economy of nostalgia at whose windmills we may permanently tilt.

But to embrace the later twentieth century (that is, to see the deconstruction of production and reproduction and their transformation by mass literacy, science, technology, among other forces) is also to listen to the voices that other movements contribute to feminism and its transformation at this very moment. For North Americans, this means paying serious attention to the claims and criticism of the feminisms now emerging among women of color. (Here, language betrays me: Stressed categories always bear the mark of inferiority, as feminist linguists have taught us. Man is universal; woman is particular. And so it is with color, ethnicity, and class. We say feminism and black or Hispanic or Native American feminisms.) Each of these experiential realities arises from the complex integrations and disintegrations of the contemporary developed world. And each lays a claim at the door of feminism to transform itself to encompass differences among women, indeed, to see female, and by extension human, identity as constantly polyglot and multicultural. All other unified, universalist notions of womanhood are suspect, for they are built to the measure of everywoman, who too often turns out to be a white, anglophone, feminist scholar in disguise. This challenge to use feminist theory in the service of understanding particular groups of women has been taken up by African American, Hispanic, and Native American anthropologists. They have examined such diverse issues as the structure of the black family, the economic roles of African compared to African American women, and the existence of a specifically female aspect to the worldwide African diaspora.[25] There is a clear picture of Hispanic women as actors in a worldwide division of labor.[26] And the specific histories and social concerns of Native American women are increasingly documented.[27] In this new feminist scholarship, there is attention on both the specific conditions and resources that women from racially marked groups confront and those aspects of their situation which they share with women of the dominant culture. Amongst themselves, African American, Hispanic, and Native American feminist scholars will have to contend with the threat posed by the reification implicit in a concept like "The Third World Woman," or her integrationist sister, "The Minority Experience." But surely, we cannot proceed any farther into the territory labelled Woman without acknowledging the diversity of women. Does such an acknowledgment explode certain of our theories? Or transform their premises? What, for example, are we to make of a psychoanalytic feminism that has bravely reappropriated the unconscious and the pre-oedipal, basing its theories on the reification of motherhood as isolated, powerless service owed to the patriarchy? What does such a theoretical orientation have to say to the experiences of African American women who sometimes claim multiple, nonbiological mothers? Or the black women who care for the children of white women for pay? Or the metaphor of maternity as part of the public, political repertoire of some African and African American resistance movements? Where is the unified mother, the universal woman in all of this?

It is in part toward these last two points—the critique of a nineteenth-century notion of motherhood and reproduction, and the centrality of diversity in women's experiences—that my own current research is directed. I am conducting fieldwork through a New York City genetics laboratory, investigating the social impact and cultural meaning of prenatal diagnosis. I look at amniocentesis and related technologies as moments in the scientific reconstruction of motherhood. Science speaks of progress; concrete groups of women may experience burdens as well as benefits from such new technologies. I am interviewing women and their families of different ethnic, racial, religious, and class backgrounds who have been offered the test, to better understand their reaction to it. I want to understand the larger context in which "informed consent" is developed. And I want to probe the cultural knowledge and resources about dependency—especially, the dependency of children with genetic dis-abilities—for different groups of women. The rationality of testing or ending or continuing a pregnancy in which a fetus is found to have a genetic disability varies according to what women and their families understand to be the meaning of motherhood and childhood. Late-twentieth-century reproductive medicine provides powerful metaphors of personhood, parenthood, and dependency. It offers a specific form of liberation that is not innocent of a eugenic edge. New technologies may have the capacity to transform the image of woman from a long-suffering madonna to a more self-centered agent of quality control on the assembly line of reproduction. Neither image is constructed by women or is necessarily in their best interests. And many groups of women now have access to a technology that simultaneously offers progress and social control. In an age of increasing scientific literacy, what women don't know *can* harm us. And what "we" know and need to know about this aspect of medicalization varies significantly along all the fault lines that help to map our lives. I do not expect an African American woman who is offered screening for sickle-cell anemia to respond in the same way as a Jewish woman who is offered screening for Tay-Sachs disease. And religion, class, and family history contribute to the possibilities and limits that potential parents of a child with mental retardation must face.

I offer this example to illustrate the kinds of problems that a feminist anthropology might address in our own cultures. For surely, science and health politics provide powerful discourses for transforming woman and her experience as mother (reproduction just isn't what it used to be!). But simultaneously, the acceptance, resistance, or transformation of new technologies of control and liberation are always localized, polyglot, and multicultural. For our world consists of concrete communities of women, not Woman, who respond to these new forces, despite the universalizing discourse that science speaks. If we can really grasp that lesson—the dialectic of Woman and women, of ideology and culture, of differences within inequalities—then feminist anthropology might help to dismantle the Science of Man and create in its place a better understanding of human agency.

Notes

This paper is a revised, English version of an article published in *Tijdschrift voor Vrouwenstudies*, 24(1985).

1. Friedrich Engels, *Origins of the Family, Private Property, and the State*, ed. Eleanor Leacock (New York: International Publishers, 1972).

2. Elizabeth Gould Davis, *The First Sex* (New York: G. P. Putnam's Sons, 1971); Evelyn Reed, *Woman's Evolution* (New York: Pathfinder Press, 1975); Helen Diner, *Mothers and Amazons* (Garden City, N.Y.: Anchor Press/Doubleday, 1973).

3. Sally Slocum, "Woman the Gatherer," in *Toward an Anthropology of Women*, ed. Rayna R. Reiter (New York: Monthly Review Press, 1975).

4. Gayle Rubin, "The Traffic in Women," in *Toward an Anthropology of Women*, ed. Rayna R. Reiter (New York: Monthly Review Press, 1975).

5. Michelle Z. Rosaldo, "Woman, Culture and Society," in *Woman, Culture and Society*, ed. M. Z. Rosaldo and Louise Lamphere (Stanford: Stanford University Press, 1974).

6. Ximena B. Bunster, "Talking Pictures: Field Method and Visual Mode," *Signs* 3(1977).

7. Beverly L. Chinas, *The Isthmus Zapotecs: Women's Roles in Cultural Context* (New York: Holt, Rinehart and Winston, 1973).

8. Adrienne Zihlman, "Women as Shapers of the Human Adaptation," in *Woman the Gatherer*, ed. Frances Dahlberg (New Haven: Yale University Press, 1981); A. Zihlman and Nancy Tanner, "Gathering and the Hominid Adaptation," in *Female Hierarchies*, ed. Lionel Tiger and Heather Fowler (Chicago: Bereford Book Service, 1979); A. Zihlman, Review of "Sexual Selection and the Descent of Man, 1871–1971," ed. B. Campbell, *American Anthropologist* 76(1974); Nancy Tanner and Adrienne Zihlman, "Women in Evolution," pt. 1 *Signs* 1(1976); Nancy Tanner, *On Becoming Human* (Cambridge: Cambridge University Press, 1981);

Jane Lancaster, *Primate Social Organization and the Emergence of Human Culture* (New York: Holt, Rinehart and Winston, 1975); Phyllis Dolinhow, *Primate Patterns* (New York: Holt, Rinehart and Winston, 1972); Thelma Rowell, *The Social Behavior of Monkeys* (Baltimore: Penguin, 1972); T. Rowell, "The Concept of Social Dominance," *Behavioral Biology* 11(1974); Frances Burton, "Sexual Antagonism and Role Behaviour in Non-Human Primates," *Acta Biotheoretica*, 1977. See also Donna Haraway, "The Contest for Human Nature: Daughters of Man the Hunter in the Field, 1960–1980," in *The Future of American Democracy*, ed. Mark Kann (Philadelphia: Temple University Press, 1983).

9. Haraway, "The Contest for Human Nature."

10. Sarah B. Hrdy, *The Woman Who Never Evolved* (Cambridge, Mass.: Harvard University Press, 1981); Helen Fischer, *The Sexual Contract* (New York: Morrow, 1983).

11. Pierre Bordieu, *Outline of a Theory of Practice*, trans. Richard Nice (Cambridge: Cambridge University Press, 1977); Judith Okely, "Privileged, Schooled and Finished: Boarding Education for Girls," in *Defining Females*, ed. Shirley Ardener (New York: John Wiley & Sons, 1978).

12. Lucile Newman, "Symbolism and Status Change: Fertility and the First Child in India and the United States," in *The First Child and Family Formation*, ed. Warren Miller and Lucile Newman (Chapel Hill, N.C.: Population Center, University of North Carolina, 1978).

13. Carol Browner, "The Social Formation of Childbirth," *Medical Anthropology Newsletter* (November 1982), reviews this literature extensively; Brigitte Jordan, *Birth in Four Cultures* (Montreal: Eden Press, 1978); Doris Entwisle and Susan Doering, eds., *The First Birth* (Baltimore: The Johns Hopkins University Press, 1981); Margarita Kay, ed., *Anthropology of Human Birth* (Philadelphia: F. A. Davis Co., 1982); Carol P. MacCormack, ed., *Ethnography of Fertility and Birth* (London: Academic Press, 1982); Shelly Romalis, ed., *Childbirth: Alternatives to Medical Control* (Austin: University of Texas, 1981); Helen Callaway, "The Most Essentially Female Function of All: Giving Birth," in *Defining Females*, ed. Shirley Ardener (New York: John Wiley & Sons, 1978).

14. Faye D. Ginsburg, *Contested Lives: Abortion Debate in an American Community* (Berkeley: University of California Press, 1989); Emily Martin, *The Women in the Body* (Boston: Beacon Press, 1987); Rayna Rapp, "Constructing Amniocentesis: Medical and Maternal Discourses," in *Uncertain Terms: Negotiating Gender in America*, ed. F. Ginsburg and A. Tsing (Boston: Beacon Press, 1991); Rayna Rapp, "Chromosomes and Communications: The Discourse of Genetic Counseling," *Medical Anthropology Quarterly*, 2(1988).

15. Harriet Whitehead, "The Bow and the Burden Strap: Institutionalized Homosexuality in Native North America," in *Sexual Meanings*, ed. Sherry Ortner and Harriet Whitehead (New York: Cambridge University Press, 1981).

16. Evelyn Blackwood, "Sexuality and Gender in Certain Native American Tribes: Cross Gender Females," *Signs* 10(1984).

17. Carol S. Vance and John L. Martin, "Behavioral and Psychosocial Factors in AIDS," *American Psychologist* 39(1984); Gayle Rubin, "The Valley of the

Kings," *The Sentinel*, (September 1984); Gayle Rubin, "Requiem for the Valley of the Kings," *The Southern Oracle*, (Fall 1989); Gayle Rubin, "The Catacombs," in *Leatherfolk: Radical Sex, People, Politics and Practice*, ed. Mark Thompson (Boston: Alyson, 1991).

18. Michel Foucault, *The History of Sexuality*, trans. Robert Hurley (New York: Pantheon, 1978); Colin Gordon, ed., *Power/Knowledge: Selected Interviews with Foucault* (New York: Pantheon, 1980). Lesbian oral history projects exist in New York, San Francisco, Boston, Buffalo, Washington, and other U.S. cities. See Elizabeth Kennedy and Madeline Davis, "Lesbian Sexuality in Buffalo, 1940–1960," *Feminist Studies* 12(1986).

19. Maurice Bloch and Jean H. Bloch, "Women and the Dialectics of Nature in 18th Century French Thought"; L. J. Jordanova, "Natural Facts: A Historical Perspective on Science and Sexuality," both in *Nature, Culture and Gender*, ed. Carol MacCormack and Marilyn Strathern (New York: Cambridge University Press, 1980).

20. Michelle Z. Rosaldo, "The Use and Abuse of Anthropology: Reflections on Feminism and Cross-Cultural Understanding," *Signs* 5(1980).

21. Jane Collier, Michelle Z. Rosaldo, and Sylvia Yanagisako, "Is There a Family? New Anthropological Views," in *Rethinking the Family*, ed. Barrie Thorne (New York: Longman, 1982); Sylvia Yanagisako, "Metaphors of Space and Sex: A Muddle in the Model," in *Feminism and Kinship Theory*, ed. Sylvia Yanagisako and Jane Collier (Stanford: Stanford University Press, 1987).

22. Joan Kelly, "The Doubled Vision of Feminist Theory," *Feminist Studies* 5(1979).

23. It is important to acknowledge the background of colonialism against which the development of the public/domestic opposition was played out at the level of theory. See Yanagisako, "Metaphors of Space and Sex" (note 21) for part of this story.

24. Donna Haraway, "A Manifesto for Cyborgs: Science, Technology and Socialist-Feminism in the 1980's," *Socialist Review* 80(1985).

25. Diane K. Lewis, "The Black Family: Socialization and Sex Roles," *Phylon* 36(1975); Niara Sudarkasa, "Female Employment and Family Organization in West Africa," in *New Research on Women and Sex Roles*, ed. Dorothy McGuigan (Ann Arbor, Mich.: Center for Continuing Education of Women, 1976); Niara Sudarkasa, "The Status of Women in Indigenous African Societies," in *Women in Africa and the African Diaspora*, ed. Rosalyn Terborg-Penn (Washington, D.C.: Howard University Press, 1987); Leith Mullings, "Women and Economic Change," in *Women in Africa*, ed. Nancy Hafkin and Edna Bay (Stanford: Stanford University Press, 1976); Filomina Chioma Steady, ed., *The Black Woman Cross-Culturally* (Cambridge, Mass.: Schenkman, 1981).

26. Maria Patricia Fernandez-Kelly, *For We Are Sold, I and My People* (Albany: SUNY Press, 1983); M. P. Fernandez-Kelly, "Mexican Border Industrialization, Female Labor Force Participation, and Migration," in *Women, Men, and the International Division of Labor*, ed. June Nash and M. P. Fernandez-Kelly (Albany:

SUNY Press, 1983); Patricia Zavella, "Abnormal Intimacy: Chicana Women at Home and on the Job," *Feminist Studies* 11(1985).

27. Rayna Green, "Review Essay: Native American Women," *Signs* 6(1980); Rayna Green, "The Pocahontas Perplex: Images of Indian Women," *Massachusetts Review* 16(1975); Rayna Green, *Native American Women: A Bibliography* (Wichita Falls, Texas: OHOYO Resource Center, 1981).

6
POLITICS AND REVISION: THE FEMINIST PROJECT TO CHANGE THE BOUNDARIES OF AMERICAN POLITICAL SCIENCE

Joan C. Tronto

During the past fifteen years, feminist scholars in American political science have come to an agreement that political science has not taken into account the experiences of women.[1] More difficult questions arise, though, when we think about why this lacuna existed and about the implications of the new body of literature on women in politics for the future of political science. Does the new scholarship on women in political science add up to a transformation of political science as a discipline?

In order to answer this question, we need to examine the nature of political science as well as the new scholarship on women. What we will discover is that a profound (and generally unacknowledged) debate now confronts scholars of women in politics about whether feminist scholars should try to accommodate their work to political science or to transform the field. I shall argue that, given the nature of the discipline of political science, feminist scholarship provides another insight into the need to transform the discipline in a radically democratic direction. Nonetheless, the likelihood is that feminist scholarship will lead to an accommodation with the discipline as it is structured.

This chapter begins by examining the structure of political science as a discipline. The discipline is, I shall argue, elitist as well as male biased. This discussion of the discipline is then followed by an account of the two ways that feminist political scientists can relate their scholarship to this discipline: either accommodation or transformation.

The Nature of Political Science
as a Discipline

Political science, as it has been organized in the United States for slightly longer than a century, is a particular kind of knowledge about politics. Like all systems of knowledge, it has starting assumptions about what objects are worthy of study and how to study them.

"Every discipline must define its boundaries."[2] The boundaries in political science are drawn narrowly around (1) the substance of political science, (2) the audience for political science, (3) the methods of political science, and (4) pluralistic tolerance. Let us examine each of these points in turn.

The Substance

Substantively, political science has three boundaries around its subject matter that make it exclusive and elitist. The first is the concern with the state. Writing about the formative period of political science, Somit and Tanenhaus noted that "Many [early political scientists] were quite content to cite Bluntschi's dictum that political science was the 'science of the state' and to pass on to more engrossing topics."[3] What Somit and Tanenhaus failed to observe, however, is that the science of the state, taking as its objects government and its officers, replaced an older political vocabulary that focused on citizens' rights. The focus on the state was an effort to move political thinking beyond its more democratic antecedents. As Daniel T. Rodgers wrote:

> Over the terrifying class and ethnic divisions of late nineteenth century America [the state] spread a wonderful coherence. Against the angry talk of rights, dispossession, and potential power seeping out of that conflict-strewn terrain, it maintained a wall of no mean thickness. . . .[4] If words are instruments, then one of the clearest uses of the sovereignty-endowed state was to blunt every dissident claim of right outside those rights the state chose to bestow: to remove the locus of authority to a sphere where the people, angry and aggrieved, could not get hold of it.[5]
> The political scientists' reification of an entity higher than the people, their axiomatic dismissal of every upstart claim against the state, their search for devices which would discern (more clearly than mere votes) the commonweal and the general will, all served to ease the recession of legitimate power from the people's hands."[6]

Even when more reform-minded political scientists abandoned the state approach in the early twentieth century, the notion of politics that they took up in its place remained elitist. In updating the concerns of political scientists, Seidelman and Harpham showed that political scientists took their task as helping government elites manage society rather than promoting democracy.[7]

Further, even when the substance of political science includes the political activity of citizens, it stops short of considering the distribution of the crucial resources that allow citizens to enter politics. Hence, with few exceptions, the economy and family have generally played no substantial part in the consideration of political scientists.

Historically, then, political science has conceived of itself substantively as a study of elites. This substantive limitation is serious in and of itself. It is compounded by rules in the discipline about its audience, about correct modes of inquiry, and about how the discipline might expand that allow no challenge to this substantive framework. Hence, it becomes next to impossible to break into the closed circle of the discipline's presuppositions.

The Audience

A second limit to the boundaries of political science occurred when political elites were unwilling to listen to the advice of social scientists. At that point, Seidelman and Harpham noted, the audience for political science stopped being political elites and became instead other political scientists. Yet, in hopes that they might still be listened to, prominence in political science still involved "speaking truth to power," and so the discipline's conception of its objects of study continues to focus on political elites.[8] As the audience for political scientists shrank to political scientists themselves, any challenges that they were studying the wrong objects or were too narrow in their approach appeared to be the challenges of the know-nothings to those possessed of true knowledge.

The Methods

A third limitation of the boundaries of political science are a set of methodological prescriptions that gradually grew up about the "scientific" nature of political science. These presuppositions again served to keep the focus of the discipline upon the objects that it had already deigned to study and to exclude new realms of concern. Despite the clear political goals of the founders of political science, by the time a large number of scholars joined the discipline after World War II, an assumption that political science was value-neutral took on the status of canonical truth. The comment made by Somit and Tanenhaus on this point is especially revealing: "Political scientists should become more self-conscious and critical about its methodology. . . . And, almost needless to say, they should make every effort to be aware of, and to discount, their own 'value' preferences in planning, executing, and assessing their research undertakings."[9]

From such a perspective, any type of scholarship that began from a clear political commitment to expand the realm of concern of the discipline would be suspect. Committed feminist scholarship would, "almost needless to say," be dismissed as unscientific.

Another problem with thinking of political science as if it were methodologically the same as a natural science, however, is that it reinforces the desiderata to narrow the scope of study. Thomas Kuhn's unfavorable comparison between the natural sciences, where the subject can simply be studied, and the social sciences, where the social consequences of knowledge make messy realities impinge, has not been missed by political scientists.[10] Many political scientists would claim that the way to make political science a better science is to make its subject or approach more exclusive, not more inclusive.[11] Thus, for example, if politics is only about authority, or if human behavior can be reduced to rational-choice analysis, the task of generating scientific propositions about human behavior is simplified. Assumptions such as only studying male subjects, defining the status of all members of a household by the socioeconomic status of the male, and so on, seem acceptable because they are parsimonious.[12] On this score, too, the inclusive and catholic approach of feminist scholars will seem to be a step in the wrong direction.

Pluralistic Tolerance

Finally, political science can defend itself from these attacks simply by absorbing these critics. As Seidelman and Harpham have argued, in the end political science pretty much accepts the values of liberal democracy as it describes such practice in the United States. And more extreme views of political reality are admitted into the association, and tolerated, while at the same time their more fundamental challenge to the discipline is never taken seriously. Such "pure tolerance"[13] is in the end a sophisticated way to ignore the challenges to the substance of political science.[14] With the substantive boundaries of political science drawn narrowly around explaining to the state how to manage the population by benevolent political leadership, it is hardly surprising that women were not considered the objects of political science. Not only were women not members of the political elite, but their exclusion from a variety of forms of public life meant that it was relatively simple to contain them.[15] Where women were, politics was not.

Accommodation Versus Transformation

Two Feminist Approaches in Political Science

In light of this history, the familiar story about the growing feminist challenge to traditional political science takes on a new light.[16] Although only two works on women in political life were published by political scientists before the 1960s, much has changed in the fifteen years since the pathbreaking essay by Borque and Grossholtz launched a profound methodological (i.e., legitimate) critique against the exclusion of women in political science. As they wrote, political science "insists upon a narrow and exclusive definition of politics which limits political activity to a set of roles which are in this society, and many others, stereotyped as male. Since society assigns roles by sex, this differentiation is carried over into political roles."[17] Thus, what women do is conceptually excluded from the purview of political science. Borque and Grossholtz enumerated a number of consequences of this starting point for the discipline. It resulted, they said, in "four categories of distortion of the participation of women in politics": "fudging the footnotes," that is, making unproven assertions about women's political activities and attitudes; "the assumption of male dominance," especially basing this assumption on family activities; "masculinity as ideal political behavior"; and "commitment to the eternal feminine," that is, "women's present weak political position is necessary and functional."[18]

Borque and Grossholtz's analysis is remarkably complete, and in a sense, current scholars have gone no further than to argue which of the four categories of distortion is worst. A number of political scientists have focused on "the assumption of male dominance," observing that the experience of women is omitted from the usual frameworks of political science (for example, among writers in American politics: Baxter and Lansing, Sapiro on interests, Klein on political participation, Mueller on voting behavior, i.e., "the gender gap," Stiehm on the effects of militarism, Kelly on socialization, Githens on "political elites," Gelb and Palley on how interest groups affect policy, Mandel and Carroll on recruitment, Nelson and Abramovitz on women as clients of the state, Kirkpatrick, Flammang, Diamond and Hartsock, Darcy, Welch, and Clark on women as members of political elites;[19] among political theorists: Okin, Elshtain, Brennan, and Pateman, O'Brien, Eisenstein, Kennedy, and Mendus, and Hartsock).[20] This focus, however, is usually met by other feminist political scientists who respond by pointing to what they take to be the much more serious problem, that is, that defining women's experiences as outside of politics (the distortion Borque and Grossholtz called "the eternal feminine") inevitably dooms the entire "male-ordered" (as Ferguson labeled it) enterprise of political science.[21]

Part of what makes the Borque and Grossholtz essay so powerful is that it can be read in two ways. Read narrowly, Borque and Grossholtz seem to suggest a problem of omission: If only political scientists would stop "fudging the footnotes" and go out and do research on the real place of women in politics, the problem would be solved. Read more critically, though, Borque and Grossholtz seem to suggest a problem of commission: Researchers have smuggled implicit sexist value judgments into their presumably value-neutral political science. If this view is correct, more needs to be done to fix political science than simply to add women, stir, and blend together preexisting concepts and ways of analysis. What may be noteworthy about this division is that it recreates a division within political science itself: the division between political scientists, who are more likely to see the problem as reparable in the existing framework with slightly expanded boundaries, and political theorists, who are more likely to see the problem with the boundary and constitution of the discipline itself.[22]

I call these two directions the accommodationist and the transformational approaches to incorporating the new scholarship on women into political science. Without downplaying the accomplishments made by these scholars, I shall next suggest that only a radical transformation of political science will ever solve the problems observed by Borque and Grossholtz. In the final section of the chapter, I shall sketch out some directions for a political science transformed by feminist sensibilities. Such a political science will be, among its other features, radically democratic and more sensitive to the broadest global and cultural context of politics.

The Accommodationist Approach

To the accommodationists, the problem of political science is a problem of omission and the solution to the problem is to generate a body of literature about women and politics within the established boundaries of political science. Although early works on women and politics had to defend the proposition that it was worthwhile to study women as political actors, a rich body of literature has now emerged on the nature of women's political lives.[23] Much of this work begins with the categories of political science and considers how women's political experience is described by these categories. In most areas, the leading premise of this work has quickly become to explore the ways in which categories that have applied to men's political behavior have to be changed in order to be applied to women's political behavior.[24]

To put it another way, the political experience of women is described by adapting categories of political behavior that have been applied in the study of men in politics.

So extensive is this literature that it now constitutes a separate subfield in political science. In 1980, Sarah Slavin became the first editor of the journal *Women and Politics*. Since 1969, the Women's Caucus for Political Science has supported work about women in politics. When organized sections began to emerge in the American Political Science Association in the mid-1980s, a section for Organized Research on Women in Politics was soon formed. Rutgers University now offers women in politics as a field of study for the Ph.D. An increasing number of political science departments now offer courses on women in politics, women in development, women in political thought. In all, this field of research is obviously burgeoning.

Problems with Accommodation

There are several reasons to think that the accommodationist approach is not the final answer to the problems of political science research on women in politics. The first concern is a problem of deciding what research is important and of focusing on the differences between men and women. Because male behavior has been studied first, any discrepancy in women's matching political behavior is viewed as aberrant and as that which necessitates explanation. For example, the existence of a gender gap in how American women and men vote has lead to a search for an explanation of why different women vote the way they do.[25] But such a search presumes, or seems to presume, that male voting is unproblematic and thus normative. The question "What is it about men who are able to dominate their wives that makes them vote Republican?" is the flip-side of the question "Why do socially autonomous women vote Democratic?"[26] But political scientists take women's behavior as the problematic to be studied, not men's. Simply noting gender differences and being sympathetic to women as political actors is not sufficient to overcome the assumption that male behavior is normative.

Beyond these problems, though, is the larger problem of the significance of accommodation. American political science is a modern scholarly discipline. Its practices are thus largely defined by the activities of scholars in political science departments in universities and by the national professional organization, the American Political Science Association. The trend throughout the last century has been towards greater specialization of scholarly practice, and the structure of the discipline has mirrored this trend. Specialization in the disciplines has been seen as advantageous because it allows each scholar, in the words of Daniel

Coit Gilman, an early president of Johns Hopkins University, "[T]he unique experience of having contributed some tiny brick, however small, to the Temple of Science, the construction of which is the sublimest achievement of man [sic]."[27] We need to be aware, however, of the ideological effect of this division of scholarly labor. In the study of politics, we must remember that what preceded modern political scientific scholarship was an older natural rights tradition and an indistinct boundary between politics and moral issues.[28] One effect of scholarly specialization is that each scholar, now responsible only for her or his own research, is no longer responsible for the overall shape of the discipline. If all scholars labor at building single walls, no architect takes stock of the entire structure. What sets in, then, is what Jo Freeman described in another context as "the tyranny of structurelessness." Without a deliberate and accountable structure for change, Freeman argued, even those with the best intentions will replicate the structures and practices that are dominant in a given society.[29] In an unstructured, ostensibly value-neutral science of politics, we can expect the discipline to take on the prevailing political values of its society. In this way, political science's central scholarly concerns reflect the structures of conventionally conceived political power. As a result, we can expect that the study of women, who are located outside of the centers of political power, is by its nature peripheral to political science. Unless scholars are able to expose this association, women will remain outside of politics. Further, those women who are studied will remain disproportionately women of the elites.[30]

What is to keep the study of gender in politics from becoming isolated from the discipline as a whole? The existence of data that suggest that women behave differently from men is not sufficient by itself to change the way political scientists think about men and women politically. As Kuhn observed, a scientific community can go about its work of "normal science" without acknowledging the importance of anomalies.[31] The question researchers who are more within "normal" political science must ask is, How will this research go beyond being an anomaly?

It is easy to imagine that political scientists will be able to accommodate themselves to the more blatant charges of sexism fairly easily. It may even be possible to accommodate the newer findings that, for example, women have different routes of political socialization than do men. But if these findings then seem to pass outside of the boundaries of political science, there is no reason for political scientists to follow them. For example, if female recruitment for elective office follows a different life plan than does male recruitment, and this difference is tied to the different roles of men and women in the family, political scientists will probably think that they can stop there. There is no reason to wonder how the roles in the family were structured, why social stigmas attach to women leaving their families to run for public office but not to men, and similar analyses.

Some political scientists may want to say, that is as far as political science should go. I shall argue in the next section of this chapter that such an approach is not a good one. At this time, however, let me suggest that whatever other weaknesses this approach may have, it will certainly not make the study of gender any more central to mainstream political science than allowing the organized section to sponsor panels at the American Political Science Association meetings that will then be ignored by other political scientists.

Transforming Political Science

Unlike the accommodationists, who see the challenge of prying open the boundaries of political science as relatively easy, those who advocate a transformational approach would require that the discipline alter its boundaries profoundly. Such an approach would require rethinking the separation of life into public and private spheres and declaring that only what happens in "public" life is political. It would also require rethinking fundamental concepts in politics, such as the notion of power. What is perhaps most striking about the types of examples that I shall raise, though, is that they lead to an increasing openness in the subject matter of political science, rather than to its narrowing. Indeed, those feminist scholars who advocate a transformational approach could assert that they want to expand the boundaries of political science so widely that the notions of which studies are central and which are peripheral would have to change.

When feminist writers begin to explore "women's political experience," though, one of the first things that they notice is that the normal concepts of political scientists do not fit so well. Inez Smith Reid's interviews with black women about their attitudes towards President Nixon showed that women were "not traditional political animals"; Diane Fowlkes's research with white women activists in Atlanta revealed that they conceived of "politics" itself differently than do political scientists.[32]

Stepping outside of the closed boundaries of political science's conceptualizations poses a different methodological problem for feminists. Once beyond the walls, how are feminist political analysts able to produce knowledge that is true and reliable? Judith Grant succinctly noted, for example, that a claim to "experience" alone is insufficient to provide feminists with knowledge about the world.[33] Hence, a great deal of recent attention has been paid to epistemological problems for feminist research to continue. Nancy Hartsock's advocacy of a "standpoint" epistemology is one outstanding example of how to cope with this problem, and it is in this light that we can understand why some feminist political scientists have been so taken with postmodernism as a method.[34] But if we keep the spatial metaphor in mind, we might be more likely to arrive at a conclusion similar to that of Sandra Harding that feminists are now in a state of a transitional epistemology.[35] Outside of the established boundaries, feminists are methodologically in the wilderness.

But if we only wander in the wilderness, then we can be sure that we will experience "experience," but there is no guarantee that we will arrive at a different or better account of political life. Methodological debates are one way to try to make sure that we remain true to our principles. But another, and much preferable way, is to try to spell out what our principles are.

As with all other systems of knowledge, a feminist account of the political will also become a relatively closed system of knowledge, best explaining the phenomena that are within the circle. If this is the case, then, the complement to a debate about method is a debate about substance. If the feminist complaint against contemporary political science is that it draws its boundaries too narrowly, then feminists had best be in a position to describe, at least roughly, how they would extend the boundaries of study and how such changes in boundaries would improve the discipline's ability to treat women in politics. Rather than suggest a "research agenda" for future analysts of women in politics, I want to suggest what type of boundary thinking might be needed.

Fortunately, several issues raised by feminist scholars already provide us with a good start for articulating what the new boundaries should include. There are two interrelated and broad directions for this reconceptualization. In the first place, political science needs to move in a radically democratic direction.[36] In moving in this direction, feminist political scientists will be able to overcome the elitism inherent in the discipline and to capture more of the political experience of women. Marianne Githens elaborated on this direction by drawing an analogy between race and gender politics.[37] In both cases, as long as politics is conceived of only in usual and regular institutional forms, the political activities of many will be excluded. Indeed, we might want to say that there is an alternative political science waiting to be developed that would look at politics from the standpoint of those who are traditionally excluded. Strategically, how does politics work for those who are resource poor and outside the circles of power?[38] I have argued that the reason political scientists have not developed such a science of politics is because it has not interested them, but surely such a development would keep political scientists busy for years. Note, further, that in order for feminists to defend such a broadening of the discipline they must defend expanded study not only of the middle-class, white, women's movement, but of "all American women."[39]

In the second place, feminist political science should question the boundaries of political science by looking more closely at the context within which "politics" appears. As long as politics is conceived as a type of activity that can be separated from other important spheres of human life, it is misconceived. Three areas of illustration will help to make this point: the relationship of politics to the family, the place of morality in politics, and the assumption of the contextlessness of the notion of power.

Politics and the Family

Since Aristotle, the study of politics has been described as the study of "public" rather than of "private" life.[40] For Aristotle, private activity included the management of the household and economic activity. Over time, the boundary of public and private life has changed, and the shift in that boundary has been the outcome of political activity. In a real sense, the "private" has always been defined by the "public" realm, because public leaders have had the authority to change the boundary of what their authority includes. Thus, to treat public and private as two separate realms ignores the interrelationship of the two realms, which is, that one is constituted by the other.

Family structure, for example, is the result of laws and practices in a given society, and the assumption of the "naturalness" of family is questionable.[41] As economic conditions change (affected by support or opposition from government), they affect family structure as well. Often, the way in which public authority constitutes private life is ignored. Thus, when political scientists treat family support or opposition to political activity as if it were prior to politics, and thus outside of the realm of public life, they have drawn the boundaries of their discipline too narrowly.

One way to avoid this problem is to force political scientists constantly to reevaluate their prior assumptions of what exercises of authority fall within "politics." Is violence within a family a political issue?[42] Is the type of almost imperceptible coercion that Susan Carroll identifies with patriarchy a political issue?[43] Insofar as the boundary between public and private can remain relatively intact conceptually, the conceptual apparatus of political science need not change.

Morality and Politics

Although Borque and Grossholtz only raised the question rhetorically, they did raise the question of the place of morality in politics. Starting from the unproven assumption that women were more moral than men, they challenged the male norm of assuming that morality had no place in politics.[44] A number of feminist writers have proposed that we take seriously "maternal thinking" as a way to reincorporate women's moral premises into political life.[45] Although reintroducing moral questions into political life would surely affect how we conceive of politics, unless "maternal thinking" is expanded so that it changes permanently the boundary between morality and politics, it may all be for naught.[46] In the first place, it is inappropriate for a social scientist to make moral judgments.[47] In the second place, though, the boundary between morality and politics is currently shaped by the proposition that morality is a luxury in politics. When faced with hard questions, political actors may have to act in ways that they know to be immoral. Until feminist thinkers suggest a way to rethink the boundary between morality and politics, they will not be able to affect this thinking.

Rather than conceive of politics as a realm above morality, it might be appropriate to ask, is there another context within which to see both moral and political action? Throughout most of the Western political tradition, it was assumed that there was ultimately a limit to political action, bounded by divine limits placed on human action. We should remember that until the last part of the nineteenth century, the study of politics in American colleges was conducted in this religious context.[48] Though the point here is not to return the study of politics to classes on theology and religion, it is to suggest that the notion of an unlimited range of options in politics, depending solely on the power of the strong, has not always been accepted as a given. That contemporary political science does so define itself points to another boundary that feminists may wish to tear down.

Power

Finally, rethinking the concept of power suggests how feminists might change the most central concept in political science.[49] Feminists are fond of pointing to the distinction between "power over" and "power to." In "power over," power expresses a relationship: A has power over B if A can make B do something that B otherwise would not have done.[50] In "power to," power expresses ability: Power is "present means to obtain some future apparent good."[51] Because "power to," often designated "empowerment," seems less coercive, feminists prefer it.

Political scientists prefer to use the concept of "power over," though, because it is most congruent with the kinds of political behaviors and political questions conventional political scientists study. At the level of legislatures, presidents, and political parties, the study of the relationship among these various power holders makes sense. If, however, the boundaries of political life are changed, other views of power become more central. Indeed, there are interesting dimensions of empowerment that feminists have begun to explore at both the smallest and the largest scales of political events.

"Power To" at the Micro Level. At the first level, feminists describe empowerment as an act by individuals and groups as they come to understand themselves as actors capable of acting, as possessing some power. This passage by Andrea Canaan is illustrative:

> I began to look at the things brown women faced with a watchful eye for a power base. What is rape but power? What is racism but power? What is poverty but power? What is sexism but power? What is oppression but power? What is deception but power? What is fear but power? I began to see the enemy as those forces within me that allowed others to control me and those who empowered or sought to empower themselves to control me.[52]

A political scientist may ask, Why is this issue important? After all, isn't the supposed power of such an actor just imaginary? How can a single radical woman decide that she is powerful? If she still cannot change events, then she really is not powerful at all.

First, this form of empowerment is important in order to explain the rise of political consciousness. Although political scientists have noticed that consciousness affects political views, the kinds of categories and concepts that political scientists use do not equip them to see consciousness change on an individual basis.[53] From the standpoint of the traditional literature in political science, the problem of socialization is to explain how citizens come to be knowledgeable about and loyal (or disloyal) to their government. At the center of the vision is the government, changing raw person into citizen. From the empowerment perspective, what needs to be explained instead is how individuals come to understand what politics is about.[54] Political scientists have asserted that it is rational for those who are powerless to stay outside of the political system.[55] In the development of a more democratic political science, it will be crucial to understand why those who are relatively powerless decide to act politically. They do so because they somehow become empowered.

Second, as Canaan's description of the power of brownness suggests, empowerment lets us think about politics in a more communal and less individual way. A doubter, wondering why one radical woman's thinking is important, would be correct: The changed "power to" of an individual does not explain much. Yet as Bookman and Morgen observed empowerment is often a community act.[56] Insofar as political scientists do not study communities so much as they study either individuals or institutions of power, they miss empowerment at its root.

Indeed, the transformation of politics into a science that studies communities rather than individuals or groups might result in a still more profound change. It may require not only that "power" be re-contextualized at the level of those who are currently powerless in the political system, but that power also be reconceived at the highest level: Are there limits to the power of political communities?

"Power To" at the Macro Level. To say that an entire polity is empowered means that it is capable of achieving its ends. This conception is a different way of looking at "power to," but it also has profound implications for political science.[57] Compare these passages on the nature of politics in a political system:

> Power corresponds to the human ability not just to act but to act in concert. Power is never the property of an individual; it belongs to a group and remains in existence only so long as the group keeps together. When we say of somebody that he is "in power" we actually refer to his being empowered by a certain number of people to act in their name.[58]

> [T]he modern state is a compulsory association which organizes domination. It has been successful in seeking to monopolize the legitimate use of physical force as a means of domination within a territory.[59]

The contrast between these two views is quite sharp and it is a question again of drawing the boundaries around political life. Weber sees legitimacy almost as a compromise between government and people; the government comes to accept some limits for the sake of easy operation. (It is inefficient to have to use violence all of the time.) But inherent in this definition of state is the implication that there can be no real limit on the "power" of the state—provided its monopoly of force and its arsenal are sufficiently well developed.

Arendt's view, however, suggests that the limits of power are bounded by what the community thinks is the purpose of the community. For a government to go beyond the limits of what is genuinely legitimate causes it to lose power, whether in the end it is able to compel people to act or not.

Although we do not usually think of power as limited in this sense, perhaps it would be healthy for political scientists to consider this question. Until modern political science displaced "rights" as the authoritative vocabulary for political discussion in the United States, there were limits to politics.[60] In older echoes in our political traditions, hubristic political actors often met with an unhappy fate.[61] Should we say that there are some political acts (global destruction, for example?) that simply go beyond the boundaries of what human beings should have the power to do? Such a question is nonsense from the standpoint of Weber's description of state power. From an Arendtian perspective, it is both legitimate and central. If feminist political science can reintroduce such questions for political science, it will transform the study of politics and resuscitate political life within the context of the ultimate questions of the good of human existence.

Conclusion

The tasks for transforming political science from a feminist perspective are only beginning to become clear. In this chapter, I have suggested that, rather than focus on methodological disputes, feminist thinkers are now in a position to turn their attention to a revisioning of political science. Such a political science will seem to be, at first, inclusive rather than exclusive in its sensibilities. The logic of opposing the exclusive quality of elitist mainstream political science requires that feminist political scientists conduct their research in a way to include all citizens.[62] Such an approach also requires that the ordinary power of ordinary citizens be taken seriously, that is, that such a feminist political science be radically democratic. Finally, a feminist political science that is genuinely true to its presuppositions will be willing to explore the broader limits within which political life occurs: moral limits as well as institutional limits.

Although this description of the tasks that remain is a long one, the good work already underway by feminist political scientists suggests that much may be accomplished in a relatively short time. Nonetheless, because the structure of the discipline and the university make them relatively impervious to these demands for changing boundaries, we must keep in mind that intellectual success in reconceiving political science will probably not be sufficient in itself. Women's studies became a field of study in American universities through political demands to make knowledge more reflective of its subjects. Until there is a political demand to make political knowledge more humane, wishes for a democratic, moral, political science that is respectful of all people may remain a wish outside the walls of academe.

Notes

1. In this chapter I shall work from my own knowledge of my discipline; hence, I will only discuss political science as it is practiced in the United States and will limit myself to students of American politics and political theory.

2. Albert Somit and Joseph Tanenhaus, *The Development of American Political Science: From Burges to Behavioralism* (New York: Irvington Publishers, 1982), 23.

3. Ibid., 24.

4. Daniel T. Rodgers, *Contested Truths: Keywords in American Politics Since Independence* (New York: Basic Books, 1987), 169.

5. Ibid., 172–173.

6. Ibid., 175.

7. Raymond Seidelman and Edward J. Harpham, *Disenchanted Realists: Political Science and the American Crisis, 1884–1984* (Albany: SUNY Press, 1985).

8. I do not mean to suggest that the study of political science is somehow inherently elitist or that no aspect of current political science practice cannot be taken in a more democratic direction. The study of public opinion, for example, can either have a respectful or disrespectful attitude towards its object. Nonetheless, few political scientists have ever escaped the gravitational pull of the powerful. See further, Jennifer L. Hochschild, "Dimensions of Liberal Self-Satisfaction: Civil Liberties, Liberal Theory, and Elite-Mass Differences," *Ethics* 96(1986):386–399.

9. Somit and Tanenhaus, *The Development of American Political Science*, 179.

10. Thomas S. Kuhn, *The Structure of Scientific Revolutions* (Chicago: University of Chicago Press, 1970).

11. See further, Harry Eckstein and Ted R. Gurr, *Patterns of Authority* (New York: John Wiley, 1975).

12. See further, Robert E. Lane, *Political Life: Why People Get Involved in Politics* (Glencoe: Free Press, 1959); and Judith Hicks Stiehm, ed., *Women and Men's Wars* (Elmsford: Pergamon, 1982).

13. Robert Paul Wolff, Barrington Moore, Jr., and Herbert Marcuse, *Critique of Pure Tolerance* (Boston: Beacon Press, 1965).

14. For example, Somit and Tanenhaus in *The Development of American Political Science* treat the New Caucus for Political Science as an organizational problem for the American Political Science Association.

15. Although it might seem that female suffrage is an exception to this point, close inspection shows that it has not been thoroughly integrated into political science at all. See Barbara J. Nelson, "Women and Knowledge in Political Science: Texts, Histories, and Epistemologies," *Women and Politics* 9:2(1989):1–25. Indeed, I would take the point further and argue that the meaning and political role of suffrage change over the historical course of the fight for women's suffrage.

16. Kay Boals, "Political Science and the Function of Feminist Scholarship," *Signs* 1(1975):161–174; Berenice A. Carroll, "Political Science: Part I: American Politics and Political Behavior. Review Essay," *Signs* 5(1979):289–306; Berenice A. Carroll, "Political Science: Part II: International and Comparative Politics. Review Essay," *Signs* 5(1980):449–458; Joni Lovenduski, "Toward the Emasculation of Political Science: The Impact of Feminism," in *Men's Studies Modified: The Impact of Feminism on the Academic Disciplines*, ed. Dale Spender (Oxford: Pergamon Press, 1981), 85–97; Marianne Githens, "The Elusive Paradigm: Gender,

Politics and Political Behavior: The State of the Art," in *Political Science: The State of the Discipline* (Washington, D.C.: American Political Science Association, 1983), 471–499.

17. Susan Borque and Jean Grossholtz, "Politics as Unnatural Practice: Political Science Looks At Female Participation," *Politics and Society* 4(1974):225.

18. Ibid., 227–228.

19. Sandra Baxter and Margorie Lansing, *Women and Politics: The Invisible Majority* (Ann Arbor: University of Michigan Press, 1980); Virginia Sapiro, *The Political Integration of Women: Roles, Socialization and Politics* (Urbana: University of Illinois Press, 1983); Ethel Klein, *Gender Politics* (Cambridge: Cambridge University Press, 1984); Carol Mueller, ed., *The Politics of the Gender Gap: The Social Construction of Political Influence* (Beverly Hills: Sage, 1988); Stiehm, *Women and Men's Wars*; Rita Mae Kelly, ed., *Gender and Socialization to Power and Politics* (New York: Haworth Press, 1986); Githens, "The Elusive Paradigm"; Joyce Gelb and Marion L. Palley, *Women and Public Policies* (Princeton: Princeton University Press, 1987); Ruth Mandel, *In the Running: The New Woman Candidate* (New Haven: Tichnor and Fields, 1981); Susan J. Carroll, *Women as Candidates in American Politics* (Bloomington: Indiana University Press, 1985); Nelson, "Women and Knowledge in Political Science"; Mimi Abramovitz, *Regulating the Lives of Women: Social Welfare Policy from Colonial Times to the Present* (Boston: South End Press, 1988); Jean Kirkpatrick, *Political Women* (New York: Basic Books, 1974); Janet A. Flammang, ed., *Political Women: Current Roles in State and Local Government* (Beverly Hills: Sage, 1984); Irene Diamond and Nancy Hartsock, "Beyond Interests in Politics: A Comment on Virginia Sapiro's 'When Are Interests Interesting?' The Problem of Political Representation of Women," *American Political Science Review* 75(1981):717–721; Robert Darcy, Susan Welch, and Janet Clark, *Women, Elections and Representation* (New York: Longman, 1987).

20. Susan M. Okin, *Women in Western Political Thought* (Princeton: Princeton University Press, 1979); Jean Bethke Elshtain, *Public Man, Private Woman: Women in Social and Political Thought* (Princeton: Princeton University Press, 1981); Theresa Brennan and Carole Pateman, "'Mere Auxiliaries to the Commonwealth': Women and the Origins of Liberalism," *Political Studies* 27(1979):183–200; Mary O'Brien, *The Politics of Reproduction* (Boston: Routledge and Kegan Paul, 1983); Zillah Eisenstein, ed., *Capitalist Patriarchy and the Case for Socialist Feminism* (New York: Monthly Review Press, 1979); Zillah Eisenstein, *The Radical Future of Liberal Feminism* (New York: Longman, 1981); Ellen Kennedy and Susan Mendus, eds., *Women in Western Political Philosophy* (New York: St. Martin's Press, 1987); Nancy Hartsock, *Money, Sex and Power: Towards a Feminist Historical Materialism* (New York: Longman, 1983).

21. Diamond and Hartsock, "Beyond Interests in Politics," and Kathy Ferguson, "Male-Ordered Politics: Feminism and Political Science," Paper presented to the Annual Meeting of the American Political Science Association, New Orleans, 1985.

22. See further, Carroll, "Political Science: Part II," and Lovenduski, "Toward the Emasculation of Political Science."

23. For extensive reviews of this literature, see, for example, Carroll, "Political Science: Part I"; Kay Boals, "Political Science and the Function of Feminist Scholarship," *Signs* 1(1975):161–174; and Githens, "The Elusive Paradigm."

24. See, among others, Marianne Githens and Jewell L. Prestage, eds., *A Portrait of Marginality: The Political Behavior of the American Woman* (New York: David McKay, 1977).

25. See, for example, M. Kent Jennings, "Preface," in Mueller, *The Politics of the Gender Gap*, 7–12, and in general, Mueller, *The Politics of the Gender Gap.*

26. How might we think these issues through differently? Consider the argument of Susan J. Carroll in "Women's Autonomy and the Gender Gap," in Mueller, *The Politics of the Gender Gap*, 236–257, who describes the gender gap as a result of the patriarchal control of women by individual men.

27. Quoted in David M. Ricci, *The Tragedy of Political Science: Politics, Scholarship, and Democracy* (New Haven: Yale University Press, 1984), 55.

28. Rodgers, *Contested Truths*, and Anna Haddow, *Political Science in American Colleges and Universities, 1830–1900* (New York: D. Appleton-Century, 1939).

29. Jo Freeman, "The Tyranny of Structurelessness," in *Radical Feminism*, ed. A. Koedt, E. Levine, and A. Rapone (New York: Quadrangle, 1973), 285–299.

30. For some exceptions: Inez Smith Reid, "Traditional Political Animals? A Loud No," in *A Portrait of Marginality*, eds. Githens and Prestage, 366–378; Jeanie R. Stanley, "Life Space and Gender Politics in an East Texas Community," in *Gender and Socialization to Power and Politics*, ed. R. Kelly (New York: Haworth, 1986), 27–50; Kathleen McCourt, *Working Class Women and Grassroots Politics* (Bloomington: Indiana University Press, 1977); Ann Bookman and Sandra Morgen, eds., *Women and the Politics of Empowerment* (Philadelphia: Temple University Press, 1988); and see further, Bell Hooks, *Feminist Theory: From Margin to Center* (Boston: South End Press, 1984); and Maria C. Lugones and Elizabeth Spelman, "Have We Got a Theory For You: Feminist Theory, Cultural Imperialism, and the Demand for 'The Woman's Voice,'" *Women's Studies International Forum* 6(1983):573–581.

31. Kuhn, *The Structure of Scientific Revolutions.*

32. Reid, "Traditional Political Animals?"; Diane Fowlkes, "Conceptions of the 'Political': White Activists in Atlanta," in *Political Women* ed. Flammang, 66–86.

33. Bell Hooks pointed to a more sinister aspect of this hunger for "experience": It is often a way for white, middle-class, academic feminist theorists to incorporate women of color in a way that does not take their reality seriously. Using their own concepts, academic feminists then squeeze in bits of "experience" from women of color. Such borrowings do not, however, a worthy theory make. See Hooks, *Feminist Theory*, 30–31.

34. Ferguson, "Male-Ordered Politics"; Eloise Buker, "Storytelling Power: Personal Narratives and Political Analysis," *Women and Politics* 7(1987):29–46.

35. Sandra Harding, ed., *Feminism and Methodology: Social Science Issues* (Bloomington: University of Indiana Press, 1987).

36. For a different argument that also shows that feminist political theory must take political science in a democratic direction, see Mary G. Dietz,

"Citizenship with a Feminist Face: The Problems with Internal Thinking," *Political Theory* 12(1985):19–38.

37. Githens, "The Elusive Paradigm."

38. See further, Frances Fox Piven and Richard Cloward, *Poor People's Movements: Why They Succeed, How They Fail* (New York: Vintage, 1979); Jane Mansbridge, *Why We Lost the ERA* (Chicago: University of Chicago Press, 1986); Angela Davis, *Women, Race and Class* (New York: Random House, 1981); and Paula Giddings, *When and Where I Enter: The Impact of Black Women on Race and Sex in America* (New York: Morrow, 1984).

39. Johnetta Cole, *All American Women: Lines That Divide, Ties That Bind* (New York: Free Press, 1986).

40. Aristotle, *The Politics* (Harmondsworth: Penguin Books, 1986).

41. Martha Ackelsberg, "'Sisters' or 'Comrades': The Politics of Friends and Families," in *Families, Politics and Public Policy* (New York: Longman, 1983), 337–354.

42. John Stuart Mill, *The Subjection of Women*, ed. S. Okin (Indianapolis: Hackett, 1988 [1869]).

43. Susan J. Carroll, "Women's Autonomy and the Gender Gap."

44. See further, Jean Bethke Elshtain, "Moral Woman/Immoral Man: The Public/Private Distinction and Its Political Ramifications," *Politics and Society* 4(1974):455–473 and Elshtain, *Public Man, Private Woman.*

45. Sara Ruddick, "Maternal Thinking," in *Mothering: Essays in Feminist Theory*, ed. J. Trebilcot (Totowa: Rowman and Allenheld, 1983), 213–230; Jean Bethke Elshtain, *Women and War* (New York: Basic Books, 1987); Virginia Held, "Feminism and Moral Theory," in *Women and Moral Theory*, ed. Eva Feder Kittay and Diana T. Meyers (Totowa: Rowman and Littlefield, 1987), 111–128.

46. Joan C. Tronto, "Beyond Gender Difference to a Theory of Care," *Signs* 12(1987):644–663.

47. See further, Somit and Tanenhaus, *The Development of American Political Science.*

48. Haddow, *Political Science in American Colleges and Universities.*

49. An interesting alternative reconceptualization of power is offered by Jane Jaquette, "Power As Ideology: A Feminist Analysis," in *Women's Views of the Political World of Men*, ed. J. H. Stiehm (Dobbs Ferry: Transnational Publishers, 1984), 7–29, who takes seriously "female" power as it is traditionally understood.

50. Robert A. Dahl, *Modern Political Analysis* (Englewood Cliffs: Prentice-Hall, 1984).

51. Thomas Hobbes, *Leviathan*, ed. M. Oakeshott (New York: Collier, 1962).

52. Andrea Canaan, "Brownness," in *This Bridge Called My Back: Writing By Radical Women of Color*, ed. C. Moraga and G. Anzaldua (Brooklyn: Kitchen Table Press, 1979), 232–237.

53. Norman Nie, Sidney Verba, and John R. Petrocik, *The Changing American Voter* (Cambridge: Harvard University Press, 1980); Ethel Klein, *Gender Politics* (Cambridge: Cambridge University Press, 1984).

54. See further, Fowlkes, "Conceptions of the 'Political.'"

55. Robert E. Goodin and John Dryzek, "Rational Participation: The Politics of Relative Power," *British Journal of Political Science* 10(1980):273–292.

56. Bookman and Morgen, *Women and the Politics of Empowerment.*

57. Hartsock, *Money, Sex and Power.*

58. Hannah Arendt, *On Violence* (New York: Harcourt, Brace & World, 1969).

59. Max Weber, *From Max Weber: Essays in Sociology*, ed. H. Gerth and C. W. Mills (New York: Oxford University Press, 1946).

60. Rodgers, *Contested Truths.*

61. Thucydides, *The Peloponnesian War*, trans. J. H. Finley (New York: Modern Library, 1951). Consider the Biblical accounts of Cain and Abel, the Tower of Babel, and so forth.

62. Bookman and Morgen, *Women and the Politics of Empowerment.*

7
A FEMALE PERSPECTIVE ON ECONOMIC MAN?

Rebecca M. Blank

Is there a uniquely feminist perspective within the discipline of economics? Although some other disciplines have had their standard paradigms challenged and entirely new paradigms developed, based upon the particular perspectives and experiences of women, the standard economic model of individual behavior has not been so strongly challenged. Although there is ongoing research and debate on a variety of gender-related issues within economics, this literature is largely written by economists (male and female) who agree on certain fundamental assumptions about individual economic behavior, but may disagree over secondary assumptions regarding the environmental conditions in which individuals operate. However, even these disagreements cannot often be accurately characterized as "feminist" or "nonfeminist" in approach.

This chapter will present the standard economic model of individual decisionmaking, then give examples of how this paradigm has been used to address issues of particular interest to women. The third section will discuss the particular effect that women scholars have had on the discipline of economics, and the final section will discuss the structure of the discipline and the extent to which women scholars have been integrated into it. Because I am a U.S.-trained economist, the study of economics is described as it exists in this country. The economics profession in many other countries is quite different in both approach and methodology.

The Economic Model of Individual Decisionmaking

The primary behavioral assumption of economics is that individuals maximize their best interests (a process referred to as "utility maximization" within the profession). Individuals choose among competing interests and options in a way that makes them as well off as possible. These choices, of course, may be limited by a variety of constraints, particularly constraints on time and the monetary resources available to the individual. Monetary (budget) constraints are typically determined by the labor market behavior of the individual, which is a matter of choice. (Desired consumption choices may of course affect work effort and vice versa.) There may also be legal and institutional constraints on behavior.

One simplifying assumption that is frequently made is that one's "best interest" can be approximated by one's total income. In this case, individual maximizing behavior becomes associated with income maximization on the part of individuals. Thus, a worker may be expected to choose to work in the job that offers her the highest wage and to seek out the best price on goods that are purchased. Although this provides obvious advantages in terms of measuring and predicting behavior, it is a simplification of the model. Although one's well-being is certainly affected by income, it may also be affected by the desire for leisure, by nonwage aspects of a job, by a concern for status, or by the well-being of other people.

Buttressing these assumptions about individual behavior, economics makes a related assumption about firms, namely, that they maximize profits. The combination of individual utility maximization and firm profit maximization provides the foundation for most theoretical work on individual and firm behavior by microeconomists.

These assumptions on economic behavior constitute the discipline's view of that much-discussed personage, "economic man" (as well as "economic woman") and are widely accepted within the discipline. However, this is not to say that there is no controversy within the discipline or that this model has not been challenged. On the one hand, those who use the model within the profession often disagree on the nature of the external environment in which the interest-maximizing individual operates. On the other hand, the model itself has been challenged, most often by those from other disciplines.

Within the discipline, much disagreement often focuses on the extent to which external constraints limit individual choices. Under the right conditions, pursuit of self-interest by individuals and firms leads to what is known as a "competitive equilibrium" in which prices and wages are set at levels that reflect existing supply and demand and in which everyone makes the best possible choices (subject to time and budget constraints), thus reaching their highest possible level of well-being. However, there are many potential situations under which the conditions for a competitive market do not exist. The result is that individuals end up with more limited choices, typically leaving them less well off than they would be under a competitive equilibrium. A great deal of theoretical literature focuses on the economic effect of such situations as excess market power, lack of full information, wage or price rigidities, market exclusion (discrimination), and so on, on individual choices and market outcomes. A related empirical literature tries to measure the size and extent of these effects. Many economists concerned about gender-related issues discern problems in the economic environment that limit the choices of women (and men) and lead to less than optimal outcomes. Others, who believe that the conditions for competitive markets are less frequently violated, observe male/female differentials and claim they are the result of free choice without problematical environmental constraints, and so represent optimal outcomes. Thus, the disagreement within the discipline focuses not on the nature of individual behavior—individuals are choosing as well as they can given their options—but on the extent to which those options may be limited by market problems that prevent an ideal competitive economic environment.

Criticism of the individual-maximizing model itself is less frequent in economics, but it does occur. Let me note two of the most commonly mentioned criticisms. First, there are a variety of questions raised about the extent to which individuals face such serious constraints on their economic choices that the whole concept of "choice" and maximization becomes meaningless. For instance, if information on available choices is extremely limited or if an individual's skills and education are so low that she cannot earn enough income to survive, then the constraints may so dominate the resulting outcomes that it is not clearly useful to think of the result as an interest-maximizing choice. In a similar vein, if existing institutions (governments, firms, etc.) establish rigid rules of behavior, based on custom or tradition, then an individual forced to behave in conformity with these rules may have little real choice. Nothing in the model guarantees an individual good choices. A single parent with three children and little education or job experience may have a choice between receiving income from a welfare program or working on a minimum-wage job. Neither of these options may appear rewarding in terms of income, but the parent is still likely to choose the option that provides the highest income for the least time away from her children.

A second criticism of the standard economic paradigm of individual behavior is that it has little to say about group decisionmaking. The whole (the macroeconomy) is simply the sum of individual self-interest-maximizing decisions. There is little room in this theory for concepts such as community or culture or society, concepts that other social science disciplines emphasize as having an aggregate reality beyond the individuals who compose them. Although a branch of economics has addressed itself explicitly to group decisionmaking (looking, for instance, at how government bodies should make decisions that affect societal welfare), this literature is not as well developed and there is far less consensus regarding its usefulness.

In summary, the economics profession uses a set of core assumptions about individual behavior that assume choice-based maximizing behavior. It is important to emphasize the prevalence of this paradigm in the economics profession, because so many other disciplines have much less agreement about their underlying behavioral models. This model, with varying degrees of sophistication, is taught in microeconomics courses from the introductory level through graduate school. Virtually all U.S.-trained economists will receive similar training in their graduate theory courses, no matter which university they attend. Thus, economists working in any subfield, from labor market studies to international trade to taxation or energy policy, will use a similar framework to model individual behavior, allowing colleagues readily to read and discuss each other's work.

It is worth noting that, since this chapter was written, a small group of economists has begun to criticize the economic paradigm out of an explicitly feminist perspective.[1] This literature is just beginning to appear and has tended to focus on the assumptions imbedded in the standard economic paradigm. Much of the criticism focuses around the "masculine" emphasis on individualism and individual control and choice. So far, this literature has not produced an alternative paradigm, but it has produced a set of challenges to and criticisms of standard approaches. The evolution of this literature and its impact on the economics profession will be extremely interesting to watch. The substantial agreement within the profession around a single paradigm makes this type of challenge far riskier for those who undertake it and makes it more difficult for such criticisms to seep into the generally accepted "idea set" of economists.

How Is This Paradigm Used to Address Gender-Related Issues?

The economics literature has paid a great deal of attention to a variety of issues that are deeply involved with gender-related questions. This has been particularly true in areas where women as a group behave differently from men, and thus the question is raised of "How can this difference be explained?" For example, one representative issue is the long-term interest among economists regarding female labor-force behavior. The enormous increase in women's participation in the labor market, and the changes over the past two decades in women's educational and occupational choices, has stimulated an enormous amount of theoretical and empirical research by both men and women. The much-cited early work of Jacob Mincer and Glen Cain from the mid-1960s provided a framework on which much of the later work on female labor-market behavior was built.[2] Thus, the tremendous change in women's labor-market choices and opportunities has opened up a wide variety of research topics for economists, focusing on both the causes of male/female labor-market differences and the conditions that have led to changes in female labor-force behavior.

The topic of household decisionmaking can provide an example of how the economic model of individual behavior is used to address gender-related behavior. A frequently cited theory describes marriage in a manner similar to that used to describe national trading partners: a gains-from-trade model.[3] The assumption is that different household members have different comparative advantages. The person with a comparative advantage in the labor market (one who can earn more per hour) should specialize in earning labor income, while the person with a comparative advantage in home-based production (one who is more efficient at childrearing and household maintenance) should specialize in that activity, and the two then share the fruits of their joint labors within the household.

Note there is no implication in this model that home work is less useful. "Home production" is as necessary as labor-market earnings for the household to survive. In addition, the roles assumed for each spouse are not based on sex per se. In a household with a high-earning woman, the model predicts that she would specialize in labor-market activity. This model also provides an explanation as to why women do more than 50 percent of the home work, even in households in which both husband and wife have full-time-equivalent jobs: The woman may have a comparative advantage in home work, even if neither spouse has a comparative advantage in the labor market. This is not a normative statement; it does not imply that women *should* do more than 50 percent of the housework. It explores the causal reasons why such a pattern occurs and thus provides clues to those who would like to see such a pattern begin to change.

This example provides a simple illustration of one particular way in which gender differences may occur within an economic model of behavior. Of course, there are limits to this model. First, it takes as given labor market and home productivity; the purpose of the model is not to explain why men may generally have higher earnings, while women are generally more efficient at home work. One would surely want additional theoretical explanations of the circumstances that lead to such gender-specific patterns. Second, this model assumes that the household has a well-defined set of "best interests," so that all individual members agree on how the well-being of the household should be maximized. This assumption means that if one member decides that the benefits associated with a particular activity have increased (say the wife decides that the value of labor-market activity has risen for her) then this should become part of the household calculation, and the activities of both partners will change accordingly. Of course, if there are serious conflicts between the desires of the wife and the husband, this model will break down, and an alternative model must be developed, which determines how conflicting individual interests are weighted in the process of reaching a joint household decision.

A second topic, which illustrates the way in which alternative economic assumptions about the external environment can lead to disagreement, is the issue of discrimination in labor markets. There are a wide variety of economic models of discrimination. The earliest such model, developed by Gary Becker, described discrimination as a "distaste" for working with minorities or women.[4] Thus, an employer with a "taste for discrimination" perceives a cost associated with employing women relative to equally qualified men. As profit maximizers, employers will never hire one worker if an equivalent worker costs less. Because it is distasteful to hire women, employers thus will pay lower cash wages to them, so the total cost of employing a woman (cash plus the nonwage "distaste" cost) is equal to the total cost of employing a man (which is fully represented by the cash wage). Although this model does not explain where these discriminatory tastes come from, it indicates how the presence of such discrimination can lead to wage differentials in a very standard economic model, in which all the other assumptions of individual and market behavior are unchanged.

An alternative theory of discrimination, developed by Barbara Bergmann, postulated that the issue is not a "taste" against employing or working with women per se, but rather a status-based concern.[5] One is happy to have women working at the same firm, one just doesn't want them in any position of authority. In this model, various barriers to entry in management jobs are implemented as a result of this status concern. Women end up being "crowded" into the lower-status, lower-wage jobs, and this increased supply of labor even further depresses wages in these jobs.

In contrast, there is a third set of discrimination models where the problem is a lack of information on true worker productivity.[6] In this model of statistical discrimination (as it is called) employers lack information on the precise productivity of any potential worker. As a result, they make assumptions about worker productivity based on their demographic characteristics (age, race, schooling, experience). If the average woman is less likely to stay on the job as long as the average man (generally true, although one might want to be careful about the reasons for it), then, if a firm is concerned about job turnover and if it assumes that any woman will display the characteristics of the average woman, it will hire all its male applicants first. This type of discriminatory behavior is grounded in either the inability or the unwillingness to collect better information on individual applicants; it may also occur if employers have false stereotypes about particular populations or if past discrimination and constraints have prevented one labor-market population from participating in the same way as another. Note that these stereotypes, even if initially incorrect, become self-fulfilling over time. If women are not given the opportunity to enter jobs that require graduate education because of an initial belief (correct or incorrect) that women's graduate training is worse than men's, then it is not worthwhile for women to pursue higher education. Even if the initial image was false, it will induce women rationally to choose less education, providing further reinforcement to the stereotype.

The point of describing these alternative discrimination models is fourfold.[7] First, this literature is an indication of the extent to which economics has seriously considered gender issues. Second, this consideration has not been limited to female economists, but much of the research in this field has also been done by men. Which is to say that it did not require the entrance of women into the economics profession to initiate research interest in these fields.

Third, these models of discrimination are all solidly imbedded in the standard economic paradigm, in which individuals are concerned with their own best interests. Although the models disagree about the nature of discrimination, and have rather different policy implications, they all use the same theoretical framework with respect to individual behavior. Clearly, accepting the basic economic paradigm of individual behavior does not assure consensus among economists about how to best analyze issues. There are those who believe that discrimination is relatively insignificant and will disappear (if it has not already) from competition in free markets. There are those who believe that lack of information or excess monopoly power or imbedded discriminatory tastes would have a serious impact on individual and firm behavior, leading to significant and ongoing market discrimination.

Fourth, note that it is difficult to characterize any of these models of discrimination as more or less "feminist"; the label is inappropriate. Although feminists are more likely to believe that a variety of types and kinds of labor market discrimination occurs, there is no particularly "feminist theory" of labor-market discrimination. There are multiple theories of discrimination that focus on different aspects of the labor market and that are probably applicable to different situations.

What Impact Have Women Scholars Had on the Economics Profession?

If women largely use the same economic models and paradigms as men, and if men have been seriously involved in research related to gender-specific issues of concern to feminists, then what impact, if any, have women had on the economics profession? There are many women economists who do not believe that there is a close link between their feminism, which determines their social and political outlook on a range of gender-related issues, and their work in economics. Certainly many fields of economics appear only tangentially related to gender-based issues (such as financial theory, international trade, environmental studies, etc.). I have asked a number of my female colleagues how being a woman has affected their approach to the discipline, and a common answer is "it doesn't." As one woman said to me, "I don't see how being a woman can affect the way I analyze trading behavior between countries." However, there are a number of fields in economics—most notably labor economics—in which gender issues are far more prominent. In the profession as a whole, let me suggest two ways in which the research of women economists tends to differ from their male colleagues.

First, women are distributed across the subfields of economics differently than men. Women are more likely to be in applied fields (labor, public finance, trade, development) and less likely to be in theoretical fields (mathematical economics, game theory, theoretical econometrics). There are surely many reasons for this difference of which I can only mention a few. First, while it is true that many men have done serious research on gender-based issues, women are disproportionately likely to be involved in fields where gender-related issues are important. The large number of women in labor economics appears to be highly related to the fact that a large number of women are interested in studying female labor-force behavior, household choices, or discrimination. Since the early 1970s, the majority of the published empirical research on discrimination focuses on male/female issues rather than white/minority issues. This situation surely reflects the presence of a significant number of female scholars interested in this topic, rather than any inherently greater reason to be interested in one aspect of discrimination over another.

Second, women continue to be less interested in or less well trained for some of the heavily mathematical and theoretical fields in economics.

The economics profession has become highly mathematicized in recent decades, and much of the most sophisticated theoretical work requires highly technical statistical and mathematical training. It is far beyond the realm of this paper to explain why women are less well trained and less willing to enter highly mathematical fields, but this tendency can be seen in other disciplines as well as economics. Note, this statement should not be taken to indicate that women do not do mathematical work in economics. A great deal of serious econometrics and related theoretical research by women is published regularly. No well-trained U.S. economist of either gender can complete a graduate education without a solid grounding in calculus, linear algebra, and statistics. However, women tend not to choose to specialize in subfields where the primary work is theoretical mathematics.

Third, there is some speculation that women are more interested in applied topics, hence their concentration in applied fields in microeconomics, such as labor or public finance. This situation is further buttressed by the fact that women appear to take a higher percentage of nonacademic (primarily government) jobs after completion of a Ph.D. than do their male fellow students. Preliminary results from a study of trends among women economists indicate that the percentage of new female Ph.D.s planning to enter academics in 1985 was 49 percent, while it was 63 percent among men.[8] Thus, one sees a decreasing interest in academic positions among newly trained women economists. Of course, it is very difficult to separate out the effect of choice from the potential effect of discrimination or tracking. Women may feel academe is less receptive to women scholars than are government or private employers. They may be discouraged by their (primarily male) professors from entering more theoretical fields. The extent to which these possibilities interact with the personal choices of women cannot be satisfactorily ruled out.

Thus, one of the main impacts of women on the economics profession has been to add to the number of scholars pursuing particular fields of study. Certainly, female scholars have done a great deal of research on gender-related issues that in all likelihood would not have been as thoroughly explored if only men were in the field. Much of the literature on issues of family, children, and women in the economy has been written because of the interests and presence of women scholars in the profession.

A second general way in which women's work tends to differ from men's is in their use of the standard economic model of behavior. Compared to men, my impression is that women are *somewhat* more likely to be sympathetic towards approaches that emphasize the role of nonperfectly competitive markets, or even to work in some of the nonstandard economic paradigms.

Among those who use standard economic models of individual behavior (which is by far the bulk of all economists, male or female), women are often more sympathetic to models that emphasize the role of market failure and the ways in which perfect competition breaks down. They are more persuaded by models of discrimination and by models that focus on issues beyond simple income-maximizing behavior. Although this inclination does not in any way place them outside of the standard economic paradigm, it does generally reflect a greater sympathy to a broader interpretation of the limits of that particular paradigm. The reasons for this situation are again hard to distinguish in any provable manner. As in other disciplines, women's experiences outside of paying markets (in households or in volunteer activities) or their personal experience with barriers in the labor market may lead them to perceive the inadequacy of individual income maximizing in an environment of perfect competition as a way of characterizing a great deal of individual behavior.

Second, while I have emphasized the fact that the vast majority of U.S. economists use choice-based models of individual behavior, there are a few alternative paradigms that some small but significant groups of scholars pursue. Most well known of course are variants of the Marxist paradigm in which economic patterns are causally linked to patterns of class structure. An alternative, which probably has a larger following among U.S. economists than Marxism, is an approach known as "institutionalist." This approach emphasizes the role of custom and tradition within social and economic institutions, as well as the influence of political and historical forces on the economy. Thus, individuals may make choices limited by traditional notions of "acceptability," learned within their families or communities. Or the constraints put upon individual behavior by firms, government institutions, or political power structures may be so restrictive that there is little possibility of meaningful individual choice. A larger proportion of women appears to be attracted to and active in using these alternative approaches. Because of the dominance of the standard economic model, those women who work within entirely different paradigms are quite isolated from the bulk of the profession (which is of course true of their male colleagues as well). Many universities have little interest in hiring economists who use these alternative paradigms, thus both job opportunities and visibility within the profession are more limited for these women.

The greater attraction of some women to these alternative approaches is surely connected to feminist concerns. In a growing number of disciplines, feminism is coming to be defined as more than a concern about particular gender-related issues. In a broader intellectual context, it has been used to provide new perspectives on individual behavior which emphasize the role of community and interconnectedness in women's decisionmaking. Feminist analysis of gender differences in economic behavior often focuses on institutional traditions that maintain historical power differentials between males and females. Although the institutionalist tradition in economics emerged long before the recent rise of feminism, this approach is clearly more consistent with the style of much current feminist analysis than the more standard models of economic choice.

It should be repeated that the number of female (or male) scholars utilizing these alternative approaches remains quite small. And the explicit label "feminist analysis" is almost never used. Instead, reference is made to the institutionalist economic tradition. Thus, "feminist theory" is virtually a meaningless term in economics. In this sense, feminism among women scholars has had little impact on altering the structure or approach of the economics discipline.

How Has the Discipline Treated Women Scholars?

I have argued in this chapter that particularly feminist paradigms have not developed within economics. From my own perspective as an economist interested in a variety of gender-related issues, I have rarely felt my analysis was seriously restricted by its reliance on the same models and paradigms used by my colleagues. However, I do not want to imply that the economics profession itself has been gender-blind. In fact, compared to the other social sciences, there is a smaller percentage of women in economics. The Committee on the Status of Women in the Economics Profession (CSWEP), a subcommittee of the American Economics Association, has collected figures on women in economics for almost twenty years.[9] Their statistics show that in 1989 women composed about 25 percent of all Ph.D. recipients, around 20 percent of all assistant professors, around 9 percent of all associate professors, and about 3 percent of all full professors. While there have been slow increases in all of these numbers, they still remain amazingly small. It is extremely rare for any of the major Ph.D. programs, which will admit classes of between twenty-five to thirty Ph.D. students per year, to have more than six women in a class, and it is not unusual to still regularly see classes with only two or three women. And as mentioned above, women are becoming increasingly likely to leave academe upon completing a Ph.D. and to enter nonacademic jobs. Why have women remained such a small group within the economics profession? This question requires serious attention.

At least one answer was already mentioned above. Graduate work in economics requires very good mathematical preparation in high school and college. Most of the top graduate programs in economics will not admit students who have not had a year of calculus and some linear algebra and statistics. Students without this background are not considered prepared for the program—and indeed would find much of the work extremely difficult. Thus, the lesser probability that women will take mathematics in high school and college puts them in a position where they are less likely to be able or interested in pursuing graduate training in economics. And of these women who do enter graduate school, their average level of mathematical training is often somewhat less than their male colleagues, which can mean that they have more difficulty, especially in the initial coursework. This circumstance cannot be unrelated to the propensity of women to work in less mathematical fields in economics.

Second, as in most other disciplines, the greatest recognition and rewards occur in the most theoretical areas of economics. Scholars who pursue more applied research often do not achieve the same level of recognition and acclaim as do the theorists. Given that economic theory is so highly oriented toward mathematical analysis, women's lesser interest in the mathematical fields means that their potential rewards from entering the economics profession or from staying in academics are lower.

Third, the emphasis in economics on choice-based models creates a general presumption on the part of many economists that one should not intervene in market outcomes (because they are the result of freely made choices). Thus, economists in general may be less sympathetic toward affirmative action programs. And the discipline's emphasis on income as a convenient measure of well-being makes some economists less sympathetic toward providing special attention to nonmonetary issues. I have been told by one of my colleagues when indicating dissatisfaction with the attitudes and behavior of one of my co-workers, "You get paid the same wages as the men, so why should you complain?" This attitude reflects a particular interpretation of the economic model, which is relatively blind to more subtle forms of discrimination and exclusion. Although these attitudes surely do not characterize all economics, they are characteristic of some significant subset which in turn influences the whole profession. This situation may have led economics to be slower about recognizing some of the gender-related problems that many academic departments have had to face during the last decade in dealing fairly and inclusively with growing numbers of women students and faculty members.

Fourth, the fact that much feminist analysis has moved in a direction that is divergent from the standard paradigm of economic behavior may make economics a less attractive discipline for some women interested in studying gender-related issues. As noted above, there is a strong emphasis on institutional and political issues in much feminist writing, with little emphasis on choice-based behavior. Women who perceive feminist studies as a separate intellectual field in itself may well believe (probably correctly) that other social science disciplines will be more open to their methodological and theoretical interests. If nothing else, the widespread acceptance of choice-based behavior models in economics makes the discipline very skeptical of any attempt to work within alternative theoretical structures.

In conclusion, my sense is that feminism per se has had little impact on economic theory or methodology. Most women in economics pursue work very similar to that of their male colleagues in the same field and feel little conflict in that. Women scholars in economics have largely not challenged the standard economic behavioral models, which probably reflects several things. First, this may partially reflect the fact that the most basic behavioral assumptions made in economics do not have any inherent gender bias. Both men and women are assumed to pursue their best interests. Although gender-biased models and interpretations can surely be constructed from this underlying paradigm, it is not the paradigm itself that creates the gender bias, but additional assumptions that may be added to the models. Women are generally more willing to accept the presence of nonmarket constraints in the environment in which the individual operates and to believe in the necessity of some market interventions to offset these constraints.

Second, it is true that many of the issues that economics addresses are not directly related to gender-based issues. Whole fields of economics, such as international trade, finance, and even much of macroeconomics, deal with issues in which gender questions are clearly secondary. The largest exceptions are the fields of labor economics, poverty and income distribution, and household behavior. However, these are a small subset of all economic issues. Third, I have noted that to the extent some women may be attracted to non-choice-based models of behavior through the influence of feminist analysis as it has developed in other disciplines, the economics profession is probably rather actively hostile to these alternative approaches.

However, having indicated that most women economists work within the approaches and paradigms of the profession, I have also indicated that there are some serious issues for women within the economics profession. Women are scattered across subfields differentially, which affects their relation to the profession, especially given their lower likelihood of being in more theoretical subfields of economics. There is also some evidence that women have been less interested in and/or welcome in academic economics than one might like, and the reasons behind this need to be seriously explored.

Notes

1. For instance, see Nancy Folbre and Heidi Hartmann, "The Rhetoric of Self-Interest: Ideology and Gender in Economic Theory," in *The Consequences of Economic Rhetoric*, ed. A. Klamer, D. McCloskey, and R. Solow (New York: Cambridge University Press, 1988); Donald N. McCloskey, "Some Consequences of a Feminine Economics," manuscript, Department of Economics, University of Iowa, December 1989; Julie A. Nelson, "Gender, Metaphor, and the Definition of Economics," Working Paper Series #350, Department of Economics, University of California–Davis, January 1990; Diana Strassmann, "Feminism and Economic Knowledge," manuscript, Department of Economics, Rice University, December 1990.

2. Jacob Mincer, "Labor Force Participation of Married Women," in *Aspects of Labor Economics*, National Bureau of Economic Research (Princeton: Princeton University Press, 1962); Glen G. Cain, *Married Women in the Labor Force* (Chicago: University of Chicago Press, 1966).

3. This model was first developed by Gary Becker, "A Theory of the Allocation of Time," *Economic Journal* 75:299(1965):493–517.

4. Gary Becker, *The Economics of Discrimination* (Chicago: University of Chicago Press, 1957).

5. Barbara Bergmann, "The Effect on White Incomes of Discrimination in Employment," *Journal of Political Economy* 79:2(1971):294–313.

6. The initial statement of this theory occurs in Kenneth J. Arrow, "The Theory of Discrimination," in *Discrimination in Labor Markets*, ed. O. Ashenfelter and A. Rees (Princeton: Princeton University Press, 1973), 3–33.

7. For a review of other models of discrimination, see Ray Marshall, "The Economics of Racial Discrimination: A Survey," *Journal of Economic Literature* 12:13(1974):849–871.

8. Isabelle V. Sawhill, "Report of the Committee on the Status of Women in the Economics Profession," *American Economic Review* 72:2(1987):401–403.

9. Nancy M. Gordon, "Report of the Committee on the Status of Women in the Economics Profession," *American Economic Review* 80:2(1990):486–489.

8
DOING HISTORY TODAY

Dorothy O. Helly

Where should a historian begin to assess the transformation in knowledge wrought by modern feminist scholarship in transforming the discipline of history? I should like to begin with a few preliminary remarks regarding "doing history" in the past two centuries in order to place in context the revolution in knowledge represented by feminist scholarship in history of the last two decades.

From Literary to Scientific History

It is important to understand that the greater number of writers who "did" history in the nineteenth century and before were neither academicians nor people trained in methods that in the nineteenth century came to be called "scientific." These writers had the professions or the leisure that allowed them time to follow their interests and the inclination to write about the past. They might be soldiers, politicians, civil servants, bankers, lawyers, or journalists, men at the height of their careers or in reflective retirement. More rarely were they women with education and leisure. Usually the purpose of their inquiries was to tell a tale that pointed to a moral, and the method of persuasion was primarily narrative and descriptive. Theirs was a literary task. Two centuries ago Catherine Macaulay, Edward Gibbon, or Thomas Babington Macaulay fit this description, as did, a century ago, the Americans Francis Parkman and Henry Adams.

By the middle of the nineteenth century, a new kind of historian was emerging, dedicated to the pursuit of history as a primary profession and a methodology called "scientific history." For these new professionals, delving into the past involved scrupulous research in primary sources, an emphasis on legal and political documents, rigorous critical methods of textual analysis, all based on the absolute presumption that, using the documentation available, they could accurately reconstruct the past. These were "scientific historians." Unlike the professional doctor, lawyer, or architect, however, whose services could command individual client fees, professional historians found it useful to pursue careers affiliated with the financial security of the academy. The university became a modern patron, with new rules and regulations set by the community of scholars who formed it, dividing their time between their own scholarly pursuits and instructing students. In practice, by the latter part of the nineteenth century the university was a hierarchically organized corporation in which a small number of male professors occupied themselves with research and writing and a larger number of lesser academic ranks taught male students who sought academic degrees to prepare themselves for such professions as theology, civil service, teaching, or finance. Only a small number of students were expected to join the ranks of the university professor. The shift from literary to "scientific" history by the beginning of the twentieth century made the work of historians in general more scholarly and less popular—the educated lay reader more often satisfied a craving for history with biographies or historical novels. The keen search for primary sources led to large scholarly projects for the publication of original documents, such as the official English Rolls Series or original writs and court decisions from the eleventh century or the volumes of all extant Roman Inscriptions published under the supervision of Theodor Mommsen in Berlin. It also led to the establishment of the English Historical Manuscripts Commission to locate and disseminate information about private archival collections. The desire to develop an ongoing means for scholars to discuss the research being generated brought into existence a new-style journal to share the results of detailed historical investigation with other professional historians. The object of history, according to the new *English Historical Review* (1886), for example, was to set forth facts, without partisanship.

Those who became graduate students in history much later in the twentieth century absorbed the message: We need only find the documents; they would speak to us and tell us all we needed to know. In fact, however, specific intellectual assumptions underlay the new scientific history. Together with an interest in the past for its own sake, there was an assumption that a study of history would aid us in understanding the present. There was a still more implicit notion that learning the lessons of the past would build moral character, a sentiment articulated as both universal and gender neutral. Yet history was first and foremost the history of political institutions, and such institutions were implicitly understood by those who wrote, taught, and learned history as masculine in character. A second assumption made by scientific historians, in their search for evidence of the progress made on behalf of constitutional liberties and parliamentary institutions, was that fundamental change was unilinear. For English historians and many of their American cousins, there was also a shared assumption about the central role played in this process by the "Anglo-Saxon race." Scientific historians nonetheless saw their scholarship as a search for the truth about the past as revealed by their sources and viewed the aim of their profession as objectivity. Because their methods were "scientific," their results must represent a single, impartial truth.[1]

The Ideology of Separate Spheres

Nowhere was the gap between assumptions and assertions so clear and the link between ideology and conceptualization of field so integrated as in the issue we today would call gender, or the social relations between the sexes.[2] Critical to the formation of the new scientific history and, it should be added, to the new social sciences emerging as disciplines in the second half of the nineteenth century was the predominance of the Victorian ideology of separate spheres. Historians are still examining the origins and impact of this ideology. They broadly agree that it emerged with late-eighteenth-century changes in modes of production and that its articulation was situated in the enterprising middle classes. As production for home consumption and market distribution gradually was removed from the household, the religiously serious middle ranks of society concerned themselves with the need to transform domestic manners and morals. Education for men meant preparation in political citizenship and intellectual awakening; for women it meant moral responsibility and learning to become good wives and mothers. Married women's domestic responsibilities were little less than the moral welfare of society. They should be encouraged not to work outside the home; working-class women who did could not help but be poor housewives and mothers. As changing family roles led to a redefinition of "women's nature," so "Nature" was invoked to assert the claim of the domestic sphere to their labors.[3]

Despite the assumption of the naturalness of the domestic sphere for women, many writers in the nineteenth century felt impelled to clarify this relationship. The poet Coventry Patmore contributed the image of the "angel in the house"; Sarah Stickney Ellis wrote her prescriptions for the "Duties of the Wives, Mothers, and Daughters of England"; and John Ruskin lectured on the large social housekeeping role of upper-middle-class women with his metaphor, "On Queen's Gardens." Even the sexuality of the women who inhabited this idealized domestic sphere received scientific definition. William Acton, writing about his medical practice with men and their functional disorders, offered encouragement to those concerned with impotence. Their problems should not delay marriage, for in his opinion ordinary modest English women lacked any sexual drive except for a desire for children. The gap between ideology and reality has become increasingly clear to gender-conscious historians. M. Jeanne Peterson found that the ideal operated primarily on lower-middle-class women, for whom it was "a dream of unachieved gentility." She concluded that the angel in the house, although much talked of in some Victorian circles, "was nowhere to be found among living women."[4]

A critical change occurred in the process of the development of the ideology of separate spheres. From a prescription that women should devote their energies within the domestic sphere to the remaking of the country's manners and morals, the ideology was transformed to a description that women were destined to inhabit a domestic sphere, separate from and untouched by the public world of men, because of their womanly nature, family roles, sex, bodies, and actual or potential motherhood. Occurring at a time of rapid changes in the material character of society, when railroads, steamships, telegraphs, and mass manufactures were remaking the physical world in which people lived, this transformation in ideology gave women the appearance of an unchanging center at the heart of existence, an unproblematic place in the scheme of things. From birth, the pattern of women's lives, analytically speaking, was the static arena of domestic life, the private world of home and family. The lives of men were seen in contrast, as spent in toil in the public sphere, as farmers, laborers, businessmen, politicians, civil servants, or intellectuals, subject to enormous and rapid changes. The public world, now identified with men and men's activities, had undergone dramatic changes through history. The private world of family and domestic life, of intimate relations, identified with women and their life-giving and life-sustaining activities, was assumed to be what it had always been. "Scientific" history and the new social sciences, therefore, were built on these assumptions, the illusory notion that the public world was significant only for men and that the private world had undergone no radical shifts equivalent to those in the public sphere. They focused on the men, events, and forces operative in the public sphere and studied change over time solely in terms of the public arena. Only women whose lives impinged upon this public arena, a few queens, a famous abbess, a Joan of Arc, a royal mistress who traded in court favors, entered the realm of high politics and therefore of the historically significant. Even the nineteenth-century recognition, from the evidence of travelers around the globe, that family forms might be different in different societies did not change the conviction "that women are, and have at all times been, defined by nurturant, connective, and reproductive roles that *do not change* through time."[5] Men, in contrast, were "the agents of all social process."[6]

An ideology is sustained over time because it is useful. The question therefore arises to whom and how was the ideology of separate spheres useful in the nineteenth century and beyond? Although I cannot consider the question at any length, I can suggest that the answers lie in many aspects of gender relations, particularly in the gender division of labor that characterized the economy. So long as women were ideologically placed in terms of their familial roles, their actual work activities both within and outside the home reflected the assumptions that underlay that ideological placement. Nancy Grey Osterud made clear how that connection worked for one group of working-class women in nineteenth-century England. Her article, entitled "Gender Divisions and the Organization of Work in the Leicester Hosiery Industry," concluded:

> Women were the secondary wage-earners within their families. Both the nature of their labour and the timing of their employment were determined by their families' needs; paid labour was subsumed by their domestic role, rather than being independent of it. . . . Their employment in gender-segregated industries and gender-typed jobs divided them from working men. It allowed the development of wage differentials. . . . The relatively low wages women earned, in turn, reinforced their status as supplementary rather than primary breadwinners, for their incomes were insufficient to ensure their own security, let alone to enable them to support dependents. In spite of their rates of labour force participation and their essential contribution to their families' income, women in Leicester were enmeshed in a set of gender relations that relegated them to secondary status both at home and at work.[7]

Women Historians

The message of scientific history that graduate school taught women historians was clear. In all the concepts of history they had been taught or were learning, in all the events of history deemed worthy of study, men played the central roles. The women historians and graduate students of history in the late 1960s and early 1970s who joined together over issues involving their place in the historical profession understood this message.[8] They were also united in the recognition of the marginal treatment accorded women in the historical profession. Women had been members of the American Historical Association (AHA) since its foundation in 1884, but until 1933 only five women had been included among the ninety-six members of its executive council; and women were consistently underrepresented on its committees in a ratio of one to nine. These statistics had prevailed in the face of the rising number of women Ph.D.s in history in the 1920s and 1930s and the fact that more women were teaching in history departments.[9] "Yet," as Joan W. Scott noted, "as the prestige and power of research universities grew in this period, women were increasingly marginalized in their confinement to undergraduate faculties and female institutions. The prevailing tone [of the profession and the American Historical Association] was of an elite male club whose formal structure and informal social practices made women secondary members."[10] Like the women hosiery makers of Leicester, women historians were still assumed at some level to be defined by their familial roles, real or potential, and were relegated to secondary status in the competition for rewards and recognition. The ideology of separate spheres, which continued to shape the conceptualization of the discipline of history at a fundamental level, continued to leave its mark upon its women practitioners as well.

Women historians and graduate students in the AHA in 1969 decided to organize; they created a Coordinating Committee on Women in the Historical Profession (CCWHP) and called for the formation of a special AHA committee on the status of women. These acts were actually part of a larger national movement among women in the academic professions in the late 1960s and, added to the pressures that civil rights and antiwar groups lent to the atmosphere of activism, their call for redress of grievances was given a forum. The result was the Rose Report in 1970 (named for the chair of the committee, a distinguished woman historian, Willie Lee Rose). That report documented the systematic underrepresentation of women within the organization and within the profession and recommended the establishment of a standing committee on women historians.[11]

Women historians and graduate students believed at first that out of the new social history whose development accompanied the upheavals and activism of the 1960s—and whose emphasis was on finding the historical voices of the hitherto inarticulate—women, too, would find their past. Instead, they found that the intellectual assumptions that placed men in the center of the questions in traditional history also placed men at the center of the new social history. The focus of this new look at the past was on workers, immigrants, blacks, slaves, and peasants, but a second glance made clear that the experiences being investigated because they were believed central were those of men, not women. A social historian at most might add a sentence regretting the absence of sources that would allow the exploration of women's lives.

Did women actually have no past? Or were they being deprived of a past as surely as they were being deprived of places on professional panels and seats on professional councils and jobs and promotions in the academy? Out of a new awareness of gender identity, out of a new determination to look at the world and at the past specifically through women's eyes, to ask new, gendered questions of old sources, to find their foremothers in order to affirm themselves, and in the end to affirm them in their own right came the wellsprings of the writing of women's history.[12]

Writing Women's History

Just as women became convinced that they must demand equity by maintaining separate advocacy groups, so historians of women sought to right the balance of male history by writing a separate women's history. This movement did not happen all at once. First the task was to identify women in the past who had played roles that were important by the standards traditionally called significant. After that, the task became more complicated. It included the reinvestigation of notable women (such as Catharine Beecher, Margaret Sanger, and Eleanor Roosevelt) by new standards of significance, reexamining both their lives and their work for other women. The quest also involved finding new ways to investigate the nature of ordinary women's lives through as wide a variety of sources as possible. Such sources included "medical treatises, women's magazines, household manuals, novels, hymnals, court records and sermons," in addition to more traditional sources such as diaries, census reports, parliamentary papers, and institutional records of various sorts.[13] When separate sources did not exist, traditional sources were "reread" for gender, for references that were there but had been ignored as unimportant or marginal. The task was somewhat like filling out a giant jigsaw puzzle, only in this case the search was for clues that might be read by piecing together information from both traditional and nontraditional sources. The aim, however, was like solving a puzzle: to put together the whole picture of women's lives where only fragments had existed before.

An appreciation of the material, spiritual, and psychological cultures women have created began to emerge with a better understanding of women's lives. Women's culture had been largely ignored by historians in the past, either as uninteresting or unimportant, but it now seemed critical to understanding the experience of the female worlds of the past. The discovery of this "womanculture" raised problems as well. Did it imply that women's nature was biologically fixed? To accept that "essentialist" position was not to move beyond the ideological position of separate spheres. How did women's culture and the social or cultural construction of gender *fit* conceptually? A better understanding of these issues required both more information about women's lives in specific historical contexts and a reexamination of the conceptual framework of binary thinking itself. Both were taking place.

From the late 1970s, with ever-increasing complexity of analysis, the exploration of difference, the diversity that has characterized women's experiences across cultures and through time, became a central focus for women's history. We have only begun to appreciate the complicated, multilayered realities of women's lives. The tug toward celebrating similarities, therefore, has been met increasingly by the demand to understand diversity as well. Doing history today entails focusing on the plurality of women's experiences: the ways women divide by race, ethnicity, and class, by age and sexual preference; the lives women have led as serfs and slaves; the meaning of women's experiences as immigrants or migrants; the different quality of the life led by women in urban, suburban, and rural situations; the experiences women have had based on the types of labor they have performed outside the home; the range of reproductive and mothering experiences women have had; the multiple worlds of women's marriage, single parenting, and widowhood experiences; the effect of geography and religion on the patterns of women's lives; how women have dealt with issues of health and physical disabilities; and what choices women have had in terms of informal and formal education.

The first attempts at women's history in the modern women's movement were not insensitive to the significance of the differences and diversity in women's lives, but the focus was on a Western, most often an Anglo-American, tradition of history. The first Berkshire Conference on the History of Women in March 1973 surprised its organizers in bringing together an unexpected five hundred historians at Douglass College, Rutgers University. Mary Hartman and Lois Banner, the conference organizers, published fourteen of the conference papers as *Clio's Consciousness Raised: New Perspectives on the History of Women*.[14] The authors of these papers dealt with such subjects as: women's control over their bodies; women's health and the male medical establishment; women's education and professional advancement; women's domestic duties, their strategies for using household technology and sharing the family's limited resources; high-ranking women's power as derived from their families during the early middle ages; women and religion in the nineteenth century; Victorian "idle ladies"; and Victorian prostitutes. Eleven of the essays chosen explored the Victorian roots of the current concerns of the contemporary women's movement. The women historians presenting papers in 1973 were generally at the rank of assistant professor or below in the profession. They went on to develop their early work into book-length publications and to be numbered among the path-breaking historians of contemporary women's history. They and those who followed them in this field brought to their work a high level of commitment, seriousness, and enthusiasm.[15]

New Conceptual Models

As early as 1969, Gerda Lerner expressed concern that historians find some "underlying conceptual framework" for doing women's history. She dismissed the "oppressed group" model for women's role in political life because her own researches had found both middle- and working-class women in mid-nineteenth-century America wielding power "through organizations, through pressure tactics, [and] through petitioning. . . ." But she believed women were to be treated as a "group" in history, declaring that women and their roles in society "are different from men. Different," she added, "but equal in importance."[16]

By 1975, Lerner no longer believed women could be treated analytically as a subgroup in history; they were the majority of humankind. She had also developed a framework for doing women's history. The first task was to add accounts of "women worthies," a term she borrowed from Natalie Zemon Davis. This task was "compensatory history." Next it was possible to describe women's contributions to, status in, and oppression by male-defined society; this task was "contribution history." The third, more sophisticated level included using the actual experiences of women in the past, through their letters, diaries, autobiographies, and oral history sources. Taken together, she believed this women's history would eventually challenge the periodization of traditional history. In contrast to her earlier statement of absolute difference, she now suggested: "Most of the time [women] have been the majority of humanity. Their *culturally determined* and *psychologically internalized marginality* seems to be what makes their *historical experience* essentially different from that of men. But men have defined their experience as history and left women out."[17] This insight is a central one. The male experience that claims universality in history is in fact the singular experience of a small majority of white, Western, privileged men. Although their power of persuasion has been the persuasion of their power, it has taken a remarkably long time for the consciousness of this intellectual fact to ferment and explode in the bottle.

For European history, the first systematic explosion came with the publication of the essays in *Becoming Visible: Women in European History,* edited by Renate Bridenthal and Claudia Koonz.[18] The book was an important contribution to women's history. The time span of its contents from prehistory to the present made the point that women were to be found throughout history. In choosing to follow traditional periodization, the editors made it possible for an instructor to use all or part of the text in standard courses. The editors set the book and its authors squarely within the context of the contemporary women's movement. These were women historians who acknowledged that the personal was political and, in this case, professional, and this made it possible for them to endorse the statement: "We, the 'new women,' are searching for a new identity with freer attitudes toward work, sexuality, family relationships, individual development, and sisterhood. We are trying to create a new social matrix that will allow, even nurture, realization of this identity. In this quest, we need to understand what brought us to this place."[19]

Beyond Dichotomy

Ten years later, in a completely revised second edition, the editors of *Becoming Visible*, now including Susan Stuard, end their introduction with the very same words. Thus the new and former authors have joined the editors in recommitting themselves to a view of women's history that marks a deliberate, conscious break from the claims of the new professional historians at the beginning of this century to set forth the neutral, "scientific" facts. These feminist historians see their task in women's history as having moved from seeking the reality behind the myths and prejudices about women that have characterized history to exploring the myths themselves "in order to analyze their relationship to the social context that produced them." As the editors suggested, "By analyzing man-made systems we question inherited moral and political assumptions [and] . . . the socially constructed and historically changing gender systems that divide masculine from feminine roles."[20]

The second edition of *Becoming Visible* reflected the nuanced complexity and sophistication that had come to characterize women's history in only one decade. One of the principal historical trends that the essays revealed was "the attempt to justify women's loss of power and authority by simplifying gender difference into a system of oppositions labeled male and female."[21] We learn from Marilyn Arthur, therefore, that it was with *polis* (city-state) life in Greece that there developed a "rigid system of gender (in which men saw women as 'naturally' opposite)."[22] From a rigid system of gender came a rigid system of domestic and public arenas. As philosophers well know, and discuss in a much more elaborate way than is possible to do here, Western thought as handed down from the ancient Greeks has categorized the world into binary opposites, that is, into mutually exclusive categories. Thus the world is made up of good and bad, right and wrong, powerful and weak, rational and emotional, superior and inferior, and, of course, male and female. Each category is a composite of characteristics that together form the antithesis of the opposing category. Bad is defined as not-good; wrong is defined as not-right; weak is defined as not-powerful; emotional is defined as not-rational; inferior is defined as not-superior; and males are defined as not-females. The sense of a natural gulf between the two categories makes them two primary principles, and this dichotomy forces other aspects of the world to be arranged around them in two mutually exclusive groups. Hence, the adoption of a "rigid system of gender" becomes a critical organizing formula for society. Either one is born to be and do those things labeled "male" or one is born to be and do those things labeled "female." And if society makes a point of the exclusive nature of those labels, what is meant by a "rigid system of gender" will automatically affect all other social arrangements.

Historians must be concerned about the consequences of such binary thinking. One such consequence is the way any society with a rigid system of gender will define what is "public" and what is "private." Feminist anthropologists in the early 1970s raised the question of how rigidly societies divided their domestic and public spheres. This question proved provocative in reexamining history in the intervening years, but doing history—and anthropology—also began to demonstrate its limitations for situations where more role flexibility has existed.[23] The need to move beyond dichotomous thinking led to the theme of the Seventh Berkshire Conference on the History of Women in June 1987, "Beyond the Public/Private Dichotomy: Reassessing Women's Place in History." At this conference and the subsequent one in 1990, both attended by over two thousand historians, the concepts of "separate spheres" and "essentialism" both began to yield to greater specificity of historical analysis and the rejection of all dichotomous frameworks.[24]

Periodization and Non-Western History

Another encouraging aspect of a transformed historical practice is a frontal attack on the question of traditional periodization. From the early 1970s, women historians have considered what history would be like if its periodization were shaped by women's experiences throughout the world, not men's. The first major experiment in breaking with traditional historical periodization appeared in a two-volume work entitled *A History of Their Own: Women in Europe From Prehistory to the*

Present, written collaboratively by Bonnie Anderson and Judith Zinsser and published in 1988 by Harper and Row. In the introduction to volume I, the authors declared: "The central thesis of this book is that gender has been the most important factor in shaping the lives of European women. . . . While differences of historical era, class, and nationality have significance for women, they are outweighed by the similarities decreed by gender."[25]

The authors went on to enumerate the other common factors they found in the research they carefully shifted through: All European women have been defined by their relationship to men; defining women's primary duties as care of the family and the home has not precluded their doing other work; women's work both in and outside the home has always been considered less important than men's work; only a few European women avoided these limits on their lives, mainly those of wealth and rank or talent, but even those have had to face European culture's largely negative views of women and the conviction thay they must be subordinate to men. Women have used various strategies available to those in subordinate positions: manipulating, pleasing, and just enduring; while the ideology of women's inferiority "was so deeply integrated into the fabric of both women's and men's lives that few questioned it."[26] Nonetheless, women did have a history, including a history of accomplishments. To trace that history, the authors focused on women's functions within European society down to the modern era and grouped women "of the Fields," within the Christian churches, in the castles and manors, and the walled towns. Thus, using these new categories and similar ones for the modern period, the authors noted that "the same historical event may appear more than once from the different perspectives of different groups of women. Industrialization affected working-class and middle-class women very differently. . . . The same is true of . . . the Renaissance, . . . the Enlightenment, the French Revolution, and the World Wars."[27] For the first time, *A History of Their Own* provided a sustained experiment with doing history from the multiple perspectives of women's lives. In connection with the historian's craft as well as teaching history today, Nancy Hewitt has pointed out how awareness of multiple perspectives gives renewed importance to comparative women's history. In our efforts to build new theory to understand the past, the necessity for analysis that encompasses a wide range of contexts becomes imperative. Historians who have been working on the history of women in fields outside U.S. and European history have compiled a useful summary of information and bibliography in *Restoring Women to History: Teaching Packets for Integrating Women's History into Courses on Africa, Asia, Latin America and the Caribbean, and the Middle East*, rev. ed. (Bloomington: Organization of American Historians, 1990).[28] This publication follows earlier efforts to make new materials on women available to those teaching survey courses in U.S. history and "Western Civilization." It includes a description of the research on the history of women that has taken place in the various fields, what has been discovered, what remains unknown, and how the information transforms our understanding of the past.

Doing History Today

Another gain for women's history occurred in the *American Historical Review*, hitherto not a forum for such work. Not only has the journal begun to publish such articles, but its editors also devoted the June 1984 issue entirely to "Women's History Today," dealing with the United States, France, and Great Britain. In 1984 both the American Historical Association and the Organization of American Historians also passed resolutions to ensure that panels at annual meetings would be balanced for gender. By 1987, the AHA program fell short of its goal by only 12 percent.

Doing history today shares many of the characteristics of doing history a century ago, when the discipline began to professionalize. We still look for primary sources, and we still try to find ways of understanding the past on its own terms as well as in the light of our current concerns. Many of the good things about "scientific" history have remained. We care about getting the details as correct as we can, even though we understand that those we study in history all had their own, often conflicting, views on what was happening to them. We still check our sources against one another, but we have greatly expanded the range of materials we consider appropriate sources. Many feminist historians no longer claim that their goal in doing history is "objectivity," but that they strive instead to reveal the multiple layers of perspectives that compose any event or moment in time, any change that involves behavior and attitudes, any use of gender as a code for defining what is esteemed and what is reviled. Feminist historians generally agree that each of us brings our beliefs into our work. When we share our results we freely indicate what we think, and let our readers judge for themselves how much our views have interplayed with our presentation. We understand that the Victorian ideology of separate spheres had consequences for doing history at the time it became a discipline and profession. The history of doing history makes us more conscious of the impact of national life on the profession and the discipline since the early 1970s. It has been important for women historians to find and claim a past for women. It has been important for women historians to find the

theory and methodology that would enable us to hear women's voices—
in all their diversity—in the past.

Women are not just another "group" in history. Studying history
from a woman's perspective is not just a matter of looking at one group
in relationship to a number of other groups. Studying women usually
means focusing on the numerical majority—but who are these "women"
at any particular time and place in history? Anderson and Zinsser began
to answer this question with their new categorization of European
women, many different kinds of women whom they place, side by side,
at the center of their historical narrative. Historians conscious of the
socially constructed nature of gender seek to find in each context the
meanings assigned and assumed, the patterns in the social relations
involved, and the ever-shifting interactions between meanings and patterns of behavior. The gain is a multiplicy of gendered perspectives that
enhances our appreciation of the past beyond old certitudes of objectivity
and scientific history.

Doing history today in an age of women's studies makes us aware
of the pitfall of assuming we know the meaning of gender in every
context; the concepts and prescriptions for femininity and masculinity
have also changed over time. "Women" may share the capacity to bear
children and lactate, but that provides only a framework for inquiring
into any society's gender system, it does not provide us with a working
definition of what it meant to be a woman in various contexts in the
past. The most recent attempt to understand the origins of the domestic
ideology of separate spheres identified with the Victorian period, *Family
Fortunes: Men and Women of the English Middle Class, 1780–1850* by
Leonore Davidoff and Catherine Hall, gives eloquent testimony to the
way English middle-class women's lives changed in tone and content
over this seventy-year period.[29] *Family Fortunes* is an effective model of
"transformed" history, articulating the changing meanings of both masculinity and femininity over time in a particular historical context. The
authors deal with a relatively coherent group of women and men in
terms of time and place, yet their careful delineation of differences
between city and countryside and within different occupations and
professions makes clear how qualified our generalizations must be in
describing the men and women of this group and their relations to their
world. If we add the varieties of circumstance that surround life in
various cultures, geographical locations, class positions, and ethnic and
racial groups, we begin to anticipate the magnitude of differences that
we need to examine to understand what it has meant to be a "woman"—
or a "man"—in historical time and place for all groups in society.

Historians doing history today must make gender a category of
analysis, but in doing so, feminist historians will continue the added

effort at placing women at the center and asking new questions from that vantage point. To do so transforms history, for gender takes its place as a critical factor in analyzing the past and as a result the past inevitably looks different. We seek not only to understand how gender encodes or symbolizes matters considered critical to culture and society, but also to understand how the sex/gender system has specifically been negotiated by women. As we understand better how gender as a system of social relations functions, we will be doing history that begins to match multiple lived realities. As we understand better how to perceive the world we study from the perspective of the women who lived within it, we make all historians conscious of the implications of gender and thus notably expand the knowledge base available. We have come a long way since the early 1970s, but we have only just begun our work. Doing history tomorrow will be even more exciting than doing history today.

Notes

1. T. W. Heyck, *The Transformation of Intellectual Life in Victorian England* (London & Canberra: Croom Helm, 1982), 143. The discussion of scientific history derives in part from Heyck, *Transformation*, 120–154. Feminists and postmodern thinkers have addressed the concept of an absolute truth and the problem of relativism in various ways. The literature is vast. Two examples only are: Michel Foucault, *The History of Sexuality*, vol. 1., trans. Robert Hurley (New York: Random House, 1978), and Joan W. Scott, "Deconstructing Equality-Versus-Difference: Or, the Uses of Poststructuralist Theory for Feminists" *Feminist Studies* 14:1(1988):33–50.

2. For a discussion of feminist historians' use of the term "gender," see Joan W. Scott, "Gender: A Useful Category of Historical Analysis," *American Historical Review* 91:5(1986):1053–1075, especially 1056; this essay is now available in Joan Wallach Scott, *Gender and the Politics of History* (New York: Columbia University Press, 1988), 28–50. For one of the earliest and still important analyses of the social relations between the sexes, see Joan Kelly-Gadol, "The Social Relation of the Sexes: Methodological Implications of Women's History," *Signs: Journal of Women in Culture and Society* 1:4(1976):809–824.

3. "There is plenty of evidence to suggest that by the 1830s and 1840s the definition of women as primarily relating to home and family was well established. But what were the origins of this ideal? 1780–1830 has been called the period of the making of the bourgeoisie. That class defined itself not only in opposition to the new proletariat, but also to the classes of landed capitalism—the gentry and the aristocracy. Their class definition was built not only at the level of the political and the economic . . . but also at the level of culture and ideology. The new bourgeois way of life involved a recodification of ideas about women. Central to those new ideas was an emphasis on women as domestic beings, as

primarily wives and mothers. Evangelicalism provided one crucial influence on this definition of home and family" (Catherine Hall, "The Early Formation of Victorian Domestic Ideology," in *Fit Work for Women*, ed. Sandra Burman [London: Croom Helm, 1979], 15).

"The key was the removal of *women's* traditional home manufacturers, which meant that mothers could no longer combine child-care and productive functions in one location and that their unmarried daughters had to find employment outside the household context. Thus, it at least became possible to define woman's sphere as wholly private and familial" (Mary Beth Norton, "The Evolution of White Women's Experience in Early America," *American Historical Review* 89[1984]:618, n. 45). The first major detailed study of the origins of the domestic ideology in England is Leonore Davidoff and Catherine Hall, *Family Fortunes: Men and Women of the English Middle Class, 1780–1850* (London: Hutchinson, 1987). Linda Kerber offers a useful discussion of the way the concept has been used in American women's history, in Linda Kerber, "Separate Spheres, Female Worlds, Woman's Place: The Rhetoric of Women's History," *Journal of American History* 75(June 1988):9–39. For the views of two political theorists, see Joan B. Landes, "Women and the Public Sphere: A Modern Perspective," and Anna Yeatman, "Gender and the Differentiation of Life into Public and Domestic Domains," both in *Social Analysis* 15(August 1984):20–31; 32–49. The history of the recent use of "separate spheres" as an analytical framework by feminist historians, anthropologists, and political scientists is traced in Susan Reverby and Dorothy O. Helly, "Converging on History," in *Gendered Domains: Beyond the Public/Private Dichotomy (Essays from the Seventh Berkshire Conference on the History of Women)*, ed. Dorothy O. Helly and Susan Reverby (Ithaca: Cornell University Press, forthcoming 1992).

4. Coventry Patmore, *The Angel in the House*, 2 vols. (London 1854); Sarah Stickney Ellis, *The Wives of England, Their Relative Duties, Domestic Influence, and Social Obligations* (London 1843) and *The Daughters of England, Their Society, Character, and Responsibilities* (London 1845); John Ruskin, *Sesame and Lilies: Two Lectures Delivered at Manchester in 1864* (London 1865); and William Acton, *The Functions and Disorders of the Reproductive Organs in Childhood, Youth, Adult Age, and Advanced Life, Considered in Their Physiological, Social, and Moral Relations* (London 1875); M. Jeanne Peterson, "No Angels in the House: The Victorian Myth and the Paget Women," *American Historical Review* 89:3(June 1984):708. See also M. Jeanne Peterson, *Family, Love, and Work in the Lives of Victorian Gentlewomen* (Bloomington and Indianapolis: Indiana University Press, 1989). The reality behind the Victorian ideology of female sexual passivity has been explored by Peter Gay, *The Bourgeois Experience: Victoria to Freud*, 2 vols. (New York: Oxford University Press, 1986). Other scholarly works on the realities of Victorian women's lives as they were affected by the ideology of separate spheres include: Jane Lewis, ed., *Labour and Love: Women's Experience of Home and Family, 1850–1940* (Oxford: Basil Blackwell, 1986); Angela V. John, ed., *Unequal Opportunities: Women's Employment in England, 1800–1918* (Oxford: Basil Blackwell, 1986); and Jane Rendall, ed., *Equal or Different: Women's Politics 1800–1914* (Oxford: Basil Blackwell, 1987).

5. Jane Collier, Michelle Rosaldo, and Sylvia Yanagisako, "Is There a Family? New Anthropological Views," in *Rethinking the Family: Some Feminist Questions,* ed. Barrie Thorne with Marilyn Yalom (New York: Longman/Center for Research on Women, Stanford University, 1982), 31. As Joan Scott put it, "middle-class men were the typical subjects acting to make things happen, while women were represented (if at all) as 'devoted' and 'faithful' figures ensuring generational continuity through reproductive roles that were in a sense timeless and therefore outside history" (Joan W. Scott, "History and Difference," *Daedalus: Journal of the American Academy of Arts and Sciences* [*Learning about Women: Gender, Politics, and Power*] [Fall 1987]:98). This essay has now been reprinted, with some editorial changes, as "American Women Historians, 1884–1984," in Scott, *Gender and the Politics of History,* 178–198. Compare Elizabeth Fee, "The Sexual Politics of Victorian Social Anthropology," in *Clio's Consciousness Raised,* ed. Mary Hartman and Lois Banner (New York: Harper and Row, 1974), 86–102, and Dorothy O. Helly, "Patriarchal Theory: A Victorian Revival," Paper delivered at the Fourth Berkshire Conference on the History of Women, Mount Holyoke College, August 1978.

6. Collier, Rosaldo, and Yanagisako, "Is There a Family? New Anthropological Views," in *Rethinking the Family,* ed. Thorne, 32.

7. Nancy Grey Osterud, "Gender Divisions and the Organization of Work in the Leicester Hosiery Industry," in *Unequal Opportunities,* ed. Angela V. John (Oxford: Basil Blackwell, 1987), 65.

8. Compare Joan W. Scott: "The experience of these women historians [holders of doctorates in history and members of the American Historical Association] as they grappled with the problem of differences demonstrates how concepts of history that posit a unitary process experienced by a Universal Man pose an obstacle to equality" (Scott, "History and Difference," *Daedalus*:95). For a slightly reworded version, see Scott, *Gender and the Politics of History,* 180.

9. Cited in Scott, "History and Difference," using the figures supplied by Arthur Link, president of the AHA, in "The American Historical Association, 1884–1984: Retrospect and Prospect," *American Historical Review* 90(1985):5.

10. Scott, "History and Difference," *Daedalus*:99–100. Scott also cited Howard K. Beale, noting in 1953 a broad set of discriminatory practices in the historical profession aimed at "Negroes, Jews, Catholics, women, and persons not 'gentlemen,'" *Daedalus*:100, 115, n. 19.

11. Scott, "History and Difference," *Daedalus*:98. She also noted that John Higham's book *History,* published in 1965 to celebrate the profession, included no works by women and excluded the names of virtually all women and blacks. See Scott, "History and Difference," *Daedalus*:104.

12. Mary Hartman stated that the goal of the First Berkshire Conference on the History of Women in 1973 was "to demonstrate what most historians, despite the new social history, have ignored: that women have a past that is worth knowing" (Mary Hartman and Lois Banner, eds., *Clio's Consciousness Raised: New Perspectives on the History of Women* [New York: Harper and Row, 1974], vii).

13. Hartman and Banner, *Clio's Consciousness Raised,* xi.

14. See note 12 above. The Eighth Berkshire Conference on the History of Women returned to Douglass College, Rutgers University, in 1990.

15. All but five of the original contributors are listed below to give the reader a sense of the major works they went on to write. With the exception of two associate professors, all contributors were graduate students or assistant professors of history at the time of the conference. Lois W. Banner and Mary S. Hartman, who argued for the need for the conference and edited the resulting volume, were both at Douglass College. The same year that *Clio's Consciousness Raised* was published, Banner authored one of the first new-style histories of American women, *Women in Modern America: A Brief History* (New York: Harcourt, Brace, Jovanovich, 1974). She later wrote *American Beauty* (New York: Alfred Knopf, 1983). Hartman later published *Victorian Murderesses: A True History of Thirteen Respectable French and English Women Accused of Unspeakable Crimes* (New York: Schocken Books, 1977). Other first books by this group were equally pathbreaking. Patricia Branca went on to write *Silent Sisterhood: Middle Class Women in the Victorian Home* (Pittsburgh: Carnegie-Mellon University Press, 1975) and *Women in Europe Since 1750* (London: Croom Helm, 1978); Ruth Schwartz Cowan published *More Work for Mother: The Ironies of Household Technology from the Open Hearth to the Microwave* (New York: Free Press, 1979); Linda Gordon published *Woman's Body, Woman's Right: A Social History of Birth Control in America* (New York: Grossman, 1976) and *Heroes of Their Own Lives: The Politics and History of Family Violence* (New York: Viking, 1988); JoAnn McNamara wrote *A New Song: Celibate Women in the First Three Christian Centuries* (New York: Institute for Research in History and Haworth Press, 1983); Regina Markell Morantz wrote (as Morantz-Sanchez) *Sympathy and Science: Women Physicians in American Medicine* (New York: Oxford University Press, 1985); Carroll Smith-Rosenberg published a collection of her essays, *Disorderly Conduct: Visions of Gender in Victorian America* (New York: Alfred A. Knopf, 1985); Judith R. Walkowitz wrote *Prostitution and Victorian Society: Women, Class, and the State* (New York: Cambridge University Press, 1980); Barbara Welter published a collection of her essays (including her famous "The Cult of True Womanhood, 1800–1860," in *Dimity Convictions: The American Woman in the Nineteenth Century* (Athens: Ohio University Press, 1976); Suzanne Fonay Wemple wrote *Women in Frankish Society: Marriage and the Cloister, 500 to 900* (Philadelphia: University of Pennsylvania Press, 1981); and Ann Douglass published *The Feminization of American Culture* (New York: Alfred A. Knopf, 1977).

16. Gerda Lerner, "New Approaches to the Study of Women in American History," reprinted in *Liberating Women's History: Theoretical and Critical Essays,* ed. Berenice A. Carroll (Urbana: University of Illinois Press, 1976), 349–356, especially 349, 354–355.

17. Gerda Lerner, "Placing Women in History: A 1975 Perspective," in *Liberating Women's History,* ed. Carroll, 365, emphasis added.

18. Renate Bridenthal and Claudia Koonz, eds., *Becoming Visible: Women in European History* (Boston: Houghton Mifflin, 1977).

19. "Introduction," in *Becoming Visible,* ed. Bridenthal and Koonz, 10.

20. "Introduction," in *Becoming Visible: Women in European History,* 2d ed., ed. Renate Bridenthal, Claudia Koonz, and Susan Stuard (Boston: Houghton Mifflin Company, 1987), 1.

21. Ibid., 1.

22. Ibid., 3.

23. Michelle Z. Rosaldo, "The Use and Abuse of Anthropology: Reflections on Feminism and Cross-Cultural Understanding," *Signs* 5(1980):380–417.

24. Most postmodern theorists have approached the dichotomous imperatives of Enlightenment thinking without a specific consciousness of the critical function of gender in binary opposites. Feminist scholars who discuss postmodern and feminist thinking are: Jane Flax, *Thinking Fragments: Psychoanalysis, Feminism, and Postmodernism in the Contemporary West* (Berkeley, Los Angeles, and Oxford: University of California Press, 1990); Susan Hekman, *Gender and Knowledge: Elements of Postmodern Feminism* (Cambridge, England: Polity Press, 1990); and Linda J. Nicholson, ed., *Feminism/Postmodernism* (New York and London: Routledge, 1990).

25. Bonnie S. Anderson and Judith P. Zinsser, *A History of Their Own: Women in Europe from Prehistory to the Present,* vol. I (New York: Harper and Row, 1988); xv.

26. Ibid., xvii.

27. Ibid., xix.

28. Nancy Hewitt, "Sisterhood in International Perspective: Thoughts on teaching comparative women's history," *Women's Studies Quarterly* 16(Spring/Summer 1988):22–32. Contributors to *Restoring* include: Iris Berger, Cheryl Johnson-Odim, Guity Nashat, Marysa Navarro, Barbara N. Ramusack, Virginia Sanchez Korrol, Sharon Sievers, Margaret Strobel, Judith Tucker, and B. Frances White.

29. See note 3.

9
THE CONTRADICTION AND THE CHALLENGE OF THE EDUCATED WOMAN

Jane Roland Martin

"Women who read, much more women who write, are, in the existing constitution of things, a contradiction and a disturbing element" wrote John Stuart Mill in 1861.[1] Mill was not the first great Western thinker to perceive that an educated woman is a perplexity. He differed from most of his philosophical colleagues in his diagnosis of the cause of the problem, however. An ardent supporter of women's equality and a firm believer that women were as deserving of a good education as men, he located the source of the trouble not in nature but in culture. Change the existing constitution of things and women will no longer be contradictions and disturbances: That was the thesis of *The Subjection of Women*, the thin eloquent volume, widely read and hotly debated when it was published in 1869, that Bertrand Russell credited with turning him into a "passionate advocate of equality for women" and Freud criticized on the grounds that "Nature has determined woman's destiny."[2]

In the century and a quarter since Mill penned those words conditions have changed. The marriage laws he described as despotic have been repealed. The female suffrage he supported has been won. The male monopoly over occupations, arts, and professions has been ended. Furthermore, women now make up at least 40 percent of all students enrolled in higher education in Great Britain, 50 percent in the United States.[3] Has Mill's analysis of an educated woman become irrelevant? Are we contradictions no longer? As for being disturbing elements, are we not these any longer either?

Virginia Woolf eschewed the logical language of contradiction in *Three Guineas*, published in 1938 but begun in 1932, seventy years after

145

Mill wrote *The Subjection of Women*. Yet she too portrayed educated women as disturbing elements—or rather, as having the capacity to be such. In contrast to Mill, who wanted to overcome women's status as disturbance, however, Woolf considered women's power to disturb a virtue. Look at people in the professions, she urged:

> They lose their senses. Sight goes. They have no time to look at pictures. Sound goes. They have no time to listen to music. Speech goes. They have no time for conversation. They lose their sense of proportion—the relations between one thing and another. Humanity goes. Money making becomes so important that they must work by night as well as by day. Health goes. And so competitive do they become that they will not share their work with others though they have more than they can do themselves. What then remains of a human being who has lost sight, sound, and sense of proportion? Only a cripple in a cave.[4]

The cripples she described "sans teeth, sans eyes, sans taste, sans everything" are not in that age of man that Shakespeare called "second childishness and mere oblivion." They are educated men. The question Woolf posed in *Three Guineas* is: How can women be educated and enter the professions and yet remain "civilized human beings; human beings, that is, who wish to prevent war?" Her answer: only by disturbing the existing constitution of things.

I want first to explain why Mill was justified in using the language of contradiction and why his analysis is still relevant today. I next turn to Woolf's thesis to see how well it survives the test of time.

The Contradiction of the Educated Woman

What makes an educated woman a contradiction? There are so many versions of the argument one scarcely knows which to cite.

"A woman who has a head full of Greek . . . might as well even have a beard," wrote Kant, one of the most profound thinkers who ever lived.[5] He added:

> A woman therefore will learn no geometry; of the principle of sufficient reason or the monads she will know only so much as is needed to perceive the salt in a satire. . . . The fair can leave Descartes his vortices to whirl forever without troubling themselves about them. . . . In history they will not fill their heads with battles, nor in geography with fortresses, for it becomes them just as little to reek of gunpowder as it does the males to reek of musk.[6]

The reek of gunpowder is precisely what worried Woolf. But if Kant seems to be confirming Woolf's worst fear, namely that an interest in war is natural to men, it is nevertheless clear from his remarks that he knew that females *could* learn geometry and Greek and *could* understand Leibnitz's and Descartes's philosophies. Kant's point was that insofar as women did "master" these subjects they would not be women, they would be men.

Ultimately, the various versions of the claim that an educated woman is a contradiction reduce to such thinking. Beginning with the twin assumptions that to be a female of the human species is to be a woman and to be an educated human being is to be a man, and adding to these the truism that a man is not a woman, the argument leads inexorably to the conclusion that to be an educated female human being is to be and not to be a woman—a contradiction if there ever was one.

At least Kant acknowledged the existence of the living contradictions called educated women. Schopenhauer seems to have viewed us as physical impossibilities. Women, he said, "are big children all their life long—a kind of intermediate stage between the child and the full-grown man, who is man in the strict sense of the word."[7] Having no sense of justice, a weak reasoning faculty, an innate tendency to dissimulate, as well as being intellectually shortsighted, women in his view could not possibly acquire the rationality, theoretical knowledge, and understanding that are the marks of an educated person. If women could, however, women would surely have the status of contradictions: not fully human because of being female, women would be fully human by dint of being educated; or, to put it another way, being women by dint of being female, women would be men, hence not women, because of being educated.

Although Rousseau suggested that behind every women of great talent a man was holding the pen or brush, this thinker who so influenced Kant did not doubt that women could learn philosophy, mathematics, and military history. He warned, however, that if we did we would suffer for it: "A brilliant wife," said Rousseau, "is a plague to her husband, her children, her friends; her valets, everyone. . . . Outside her home she is always ridiculous and very justly criticized."[8] Yet the hardships an educated woman is bound to experience were not his real concern. Like Kant, Rousseau represented her as a violation of nature: "Believe me, judicious mother, do not make a decent man of your daughter, as though you would give nature the lie."[9]

Mill did not for a moment think that a woman who could read and write, let alone do philosophy and mathematics, violated nature. On the contrary, he rejected this idea, saying: "I deny that anyone knows, or can know, the nature of the two sexes, as long as they have only been seen in their present relation to one another." Yet he did not call educated women contradictions simply to remind his readers how others saw them. Mill understood that man and woman are social, psychological, and cultural as well as biological categories and that different cultural and social norms govern the two sexes. Thus, while others were maintaining that Nature circumscribes women's abilities and prescribes her place in society, Mill insisted that these limits were set by culture. "What is now called the nature of women is an eminently artificial thing—the result of forced repression in some directions, unnatural stimulation in others,"[10] he wrote. Artificial or natural, so long as education fosters "manly" qualities and these are taken to be the polar opposites of "womanly" ones, educated women will constitute contradictions.

To accommodate educated women—to resolve our contradictory status—Mill wanted to reform society. Rousseau, Kant, and Schopenhauer would have no accommodations made. Cultivate woman's and only woman's qualities in society's daughters, Rousseau in effect told readers of Book V of *Emile*, and they will be neither disturbances nor living contradictions. I need hardly say here that this solution to the problem of educated woman as contradiction is unacceptable. Barring women from the very kind of education required of citizens in a democracy and denying them the traits and capacities considered the mark of a moral individual, Rousseau insured our second-class status both at home and in the world.

We must not think, however, that because Mill's analysis is acute and his heart is in the right place, we should accept unquestioningly his solution to educated women's contradictory status, that of providing freer access to an education originally designed for boys and men and changing cultural attitudes toward women knowing geometry and thinking abstractly. Over the years most women and men who have believed in women's rights and the equality of the sexes have adopted the first part of Mill's program—demanding and fighting for the extension to girls and women of the curriculum studied by the educated men in their midst. Too few, however, have perceived the dilemma for women inherent in the achievement of this goal. Thus, until the advent of women's studies programs in our schools, colleges, and universities, the "degenderization" of the qualities built into our cultural concept of an educated person, by which I mean the detaching of them from our cultural construct of masculinity, has seldom been a designated aim of education, and even now it is rarely acknowledged as such.

Make no mistake. Although there are many more qualities our society considers to be a man's than those belonging to our conception of an educated person, and although many men by virtue of their race or class have been thought to be lacking in just these dimensions, the traits we take to be the marks of an educated individual are the very ones that Rousseau, Kant, and Schopenhauer assigned to men by nature and that Mill knew were denied women by culture. Rationality, a highly developed capacity for abstract analytic thought, self-government, independence: These were considered in Mill's England to be a "man's qualities" hence not "a woman's," and they are still perceived in this way by many in the United States.

I do not for a moment mean to suggest that it was wrong for Mill to want to appropriate for England's daughters the education of its sons. This effort was seen by him, as by its adherents in this country, to be a necessary step in ending the subordination of women.[11] However, we need to understand the framework of assumptions about gender within which this program of appropriation operates, for the conjunction of the two creates people who, as living contradictions, may even today have special educational problems and needs.[12]

The Need for a Gender-Sensitive
Ideal of the Educated Person

According to a recent report of the Organization for Economic Cooperation and Development (OECD),[13] in Canada, Finland, France, and the United States, women make up at least half of all students enrolled in higher education. In most other industrialized Western countries they make up at least 40 percent. Yet the report cautioned against complacency over the status of women in higher education. Recognizing that educational equality is not simply a matter of equal admissions, it noted that more males than females attain the top scholarships and the postgraduate degrees. It noted too that fields of study are sharply divided by sex. On the face of it, this discrepancy might seem unobjectionable. Surely the ideal of equality does not require that every subject be taken by equal numbers of females and males. The report makes it clear, however, that the subjects in which females predominate are the very ones in which job opportunities have been severely curtailed in recent years and, moreover, that these fields are presently at risk of being downgraded in academic standing and resources.

Given the fact of equal access to higher education, why does there seem to be a marked difference in male and female achievement? Why does the same education for the two sexes not yield the same results? Mill's insight into the genderization of the traits associated with "true" education and the consequent contradictory status of an educated woman is relevant here.

Research in coeducational classrooms and their surrounding environments shows that when what was originally a boy's or young man's education is extended to girls and women and the two sexes are educated together, the educational treatment of the sexes will not necessarily be the same.[14] Furthermore, even when the treatment itself is the same, it is frequently experienced differently. I want to stress that different educational treatment of females and males is not in itself suspect. Studies of the coeducational classroom climate are important not because they have uncovered differences where none were thought to exist, but because the differences uncovered are so damaging to women. When you feel peripheral in class, when your participation is not expected and your contributions are not thought to be important, it will scarcely be surprising if you begin to doubt your own intellectual capacity. Nor will it be surprising if, when your academic achievements are minimized and your career goals are not taken seriously, you lose your self-confidence.

With even the best will in the world, it is not easy to achieve identical treatment of males and females in coeducational classrooms.[15] But supposing we could readily achieve it, we must ask ourselves if identical treatment should be our goal. The hypothesis that the same education for both sexes will yield the same results rests on the assumption that sex is a difference that makes no difference.[16] By all means let us side with Mill against philosophers such as Rousseau, Kant, and Schopenhauer in extending the duties, tasks, and privileges of citizenship to women. But let us not, therefore, suppose that gender is irrelevant to education. In the first place, people with similar talents who might be expected to perform the same tasks with equal proficiency often learn in different ways, thereby benefiting from different modes of instruction. Furthermore, some start with handicaps, having nothing to do with natural aptitude, that must be overcome if a given end is to be achieved. In either case it is a mistake to assume that an identical education will yield identical results in all instances.

The question, of course, is whether differences in learning styles and learning readiness are systematically related to gender. To ask this question is not to raise the specter of biological determinism. We who are committed to the ideal of sex equality must remember that whether or not identical results require identical educational treatment is an *empirical* question, and that until the necessary research on gender and learning is done, a healthy skepticism must be maintained toward the postulate that the same societal role requires the same education.

Such skepticism is particularly warranted in light of the literature on the socialization of boys and girls.[17] Treated differently from birth, and with different expectations held up to them within the family and in the early years of schooling, children become aware at an early age of their culture's distinctions between masculine and feminine roles and of their culture's higher valuation of men and masculine roles. This process of socialization, begun in infancy, continues through childhood and adolescence into adulthood. Would it not be astonishing if it had no consequences for learning?

Given that any acknowledgment of the workings of gender in education is likely to be construed as an acceptance of fixed male and female natures, it is tempting to adopt the strategy of ignoring gender entirely. Yet the phenomenon of *trait genderization* invalidates this tactic. As Mill realized, many qualities are genderized—that is appraised differently by a given culture or society when possessed by males and females.[18] Aggressiveness, for example, is judged in North America, at least, to be a desirable trait for males, but not females, to possess. So, too, a highly developed capacity for abstract reasoning, a self-control in which feeling and emotion are subordinated to the rule of reason, and an independent spirit are qualities for which men are praised and women are regarded with suspicion, if not downright disdain.[19] Yet these latter are the very qualities an educated woman is supposed to possess.

In the face of the trait genderization embedded in our culture, the dictum that sex or gender is a difference of no consequence to education loses credibility. If in order to become truly educated people those born female must acquire the very "man's qualities" for which they are denigrated, will not this negative evaluation reverberate in the way and the extent to which the traits are acquired? No one who has been moved by Mill's arguments in favor of the education of female reason and self-government could possibly want to seal off women's education from every quality genderized in favor of males. Yet in rejecting a gender-bound educational philosophy like Rousseau's, let us not forget what Mill knew, namely that traits and gender are related. And let us not ignore the growing literature that shows gender to be a significant dimension of life in classrooms.

"Educational equality between the sexes is still far from having been realized," the OECD report says. I fear that as long as women's education is designed on the one hand to develop traits genderized in favor of males and on the other to ignore gender differences related to learning, this finding will continue to hold true. In the name of identical educational treatment girls and women will experience difficulties and suffer hardships their male counterparts will never know. But if identical treatment is untenable, if, indeed, it gives us the illusion of gender-neutrality whereas in fact it intensifies the problems of becoming an educated woman, what is to be done?

There is an alternative to the dictum that sex is a difference that makes no difference that does not commit us to a regressive two-track educational system based on sex. Joining Mill's insights that traits and gender are connected and that roles and gender are not fixed by nature,[20] we can adopt a *gender-sensitive* ideal as opposed to either an illusory gender-free one or a vicious gender-bound one. Taking gender into account when it makes a difference and ignoring it when it does not, a gender-sensitive ideal allows educators to build into curricula, instructional methods, and learning environments ways of dealing with trait genderization and with the many and various other gender-related phenomena—for example, the portrayals of women in the subject matter of the curriculum—that enter into education today.

In acknowledging gender without making us its prisoners, a gender-sensitive ideal allows us to continue Mill's project of building into the education of females traits genderized in favor of males without victimizing women. It also makes possible Virginia Woolf's more revolutionary and absolutely essential project.

The View from the Bridge

If any single image dominates Woolf's *Three Guineas*, it is a bridge connecting two worlds: public and private, home and professions, women's and men's. Woolf invites us in imagination to see "the educated man's daughter"—the woman she was writing about—"as she issues from the shadow of the private house, and starts on the bridge which lies between the old world and the new" (p. 16). She then laid before her male readers "a photograph . . . of your world as it appears to us who see it from the threshold of the private house . . . from the bridge which connects the private house with the world of public life" (p. 18). Asking how to educate the young to hate war, she asked that women "turn from our station on the bridge across the Thames to another bridge over another river, this time in one of the great universities. Once more, how strange it looks, this world of domes and spires, of lecture rooms and laboratories, from our vantage point! How different it must look to you!" (p. 23). Finally, calling women back to the bridge over the Thames, she told them to "fix our eyes upon the procession—the procession of the sons of educated men" (p. 60).

"There they go," Woolf said,

> our brothers who have been educated in public schools and universities, mounting those steps, passing in and out of those doors, ascending those pulpits, preaching, teaching, administering justice, practising medicine, trans-

acting business, making money. It is a solemn sight always. . . . But now, for the past twenty years or so, it is no longer a sight merely, a photograph, or fresco scrawled upon the walls of time, at which we can look with merely an esthetic appreciation. For there trapesing along at the tail end of the procession, we go ourselves (pp. 60–61).

Watching this procession march into the city and speaking this time to her female readers, she said, "We have to ask ourselves, here and now, do we wish to join the procession, or don't we? On what terms shall we join the procession? Above all, where is it leading us, the procession of educated men?" (p. 62). Her answer took the form of more questions. Insisting that the professions make those who practice them "possessive, jealous of any infringement of their rights, and highly combative if anyone dares dispute them," Woolf asked:

Are we not right then in thinking that if we enter the same professions we shall acquire the same qualities? And do not such qualities lead to war? In another century or so if we practise the professions in the same way, shall we not be just as possessive, just as jealous, just as pugnacious, just as positive as to the verdict of God, Nature, Law and Property as these gentlemen are now? (p. 66).

Woolf's eye for the vanities of dress and distinctions of rank in the then-male bastions of the bar, the church, the stock exchange, the civil service, medicine, publishing was merciless. Her perceptions of the connection between these professions and war chill the blood. Yet despite the fact that she has been called a "separatist,"[21] she did not answer her own question by telling women to keep out for she perceived that the daughters of educated men "are between the devil and the deep blue sea": "Behind us lies the patriarchal system, the private house, with its nullity, its immorality, its hypocrisy, its servility. Before us lies the public world, the professional system, with its possessiveness, its jealousy, its pugnacity, its greed" (p. 74). "Had we not better plunge off the bridge into the river; give up the game; declare that the whole of human life is a mistake and so end it?" asked Woolf who three years after the publication of *Three Guineas* took her own life by walking into the water. No, she said, there is another course open.

From reading biographies of educated women who had entered the public world and managed to remain civilized, Woolf discovered that what Florence Nightingale and the others all shared was instruction from teachers their brothers never knew. Poverty, chastity, derision, and freedom from unreal loyalties she called them; not pretty names, but she tempered their impact by redefining their scope. Rather than being destitution, "poverty" is "enough money to live upon. . . . But no more. Not a penny more." "Chastity" does not refer to sexual abstinence but means, "when you have made enough to live on by your profession you must refuse to sell your brain for the sake of money." "Derision"— she admitted it was a bad word for what she had in mind—means that "you must refuse all methods of advertising merit, and hold that ridicule, obscurity and censure are preferable, for psychological reasons, to fame and praise." And freedom from unreal loyalties means "you must rid yourself of pride of nationality in the first place; also of religious pride, college pride, school pride, family pride, sex pride and the unreal loyalties that spring from them." Agree to live by these terms and one other, namely "that you help all properly qualified people, of whatever sex, class or colour, to enter your profession" (p. 80), Woolf said to women, and "you can join the professions and yet remain uncontaminated by them; you can rid them of their possessiveness, their jealousy, their pugnacity, their greed. You can use them to have a mind of your own and a will of your own. And you can use that mind and will to abolish the inhumanity, the beastliness, the horror, the folly of war" (p. 83).

Mill was the one who said that women who read and write are a disturbing element as well as a contradiction, but he did not think they disrupted the social order. Rousseau did. He feared that if a woman was a scholar or accountant, a soldier or diplomat, she would perform her "women's duties" badly or, worse still, neglect them altogether. Hegel, one of Rousseau's direct descendents, went so far as to say, "When women hold the helm of government, the State is at once in jeopardy."[22] Schopenhauer, in turn, wondered if the influence of women on the French court and government did not hasten the Revolution. Like these traditionalists, Woolf saw educated women—at least those trained by her four teachers—as bearers of disorder. But she invested women's power to disarrange the existing constitution of things with positive value.

In the last scene of the play *Wild Honey*, Chekhov had Anna Petrovna say:

> It's terrible to be an educated woman. An educated woman with nothing to do. What am I here for? Why am I alive? . . . They should make me a professor somewhere, or a director of something. . . . If I were a diplomat I'd turn the whole world upside down. . . . An educated woman . . . And nothing to do. So I'm no use. Horses, cows, dogs—they all have their uses. Not me, though. I'm irrelevant.[23]

Her self-revelation is painful, not the least because through the play's action the audience has come to know Anna Petrovna as the linchpin of the small society gathered on her decaying estate. Occupied not only in trying to save the family home from its creditors but also in soothing tempers and mending fractured relationships, she is surely the least idle, least irrelevant of the play's many characters. What matters, however, is her view of herself: her feelings of failure, her sense of despair, her perception of the mismatch between the life for which her education prepared her and the one she had actually to live, and also her momentary vision of what she might have accomplished.

Anna Petrovna's dream of herself as a diplomat who would turn the whole world upside down is Virginia Woolf's dream for educated women as a group. With respect to war, the Woolf of *Three Guineas* is indeed a separatist: Have nothing at all to do with it, she told women. But with respect to the professions she is not. She would have women join the procession across the bridge and enter the city of professions *on condition that in so doing they remake man's culture.*

The City on the Hillside

More than fifty years have elapsed since Woolf bid women join her on the bridge. Does man's culture still need to be remade? In the United States, violence at home and in our public spaces is rife. In the world at large, war has become even more deadly than Woolf knew it to be. And besides the promise of quick destruction to all living creatures of the nuclear peril born of that war whose end Woolf did not wait to see, we now face the equally grave—possibly far graver—danger of a slow, lingering, planetary death brought on by the human species' arrogant disregard for its earthly surroundings.

Have educated women become "just as possessive, just as jealous, just as pugnacious, just as positive as to the verdict of God, Nature, Law and Property" as Woolf said professional men were in half the time she predicted it would take them? Or, remaining civilized human beings, are they the disturbing elements that Woolf wanted them to be and that our own upside down world so sorely needs? Come stand on the bridge with me and watch the procession circa 1990.

Look at all those women! They are not just traipsing along at the end as they were in the 1930s. See the ones marching at the head. They are as solemn as the men and seem almost as confident. True, they do not walk as freely. Is that because their gray suits have skirts not trousers and their heels are high? And what do you suppose is wrong with the woman over there? She appears to be distraught. You say her child is sick? That she is wondering how to sandwich in a trip to the doctor between clients? But Woolf led us to understand that the daughters and sisters of educated men had the choice of staying in the private, patriarchal home to practice the unpaid professions of marriage and mothering or entering the uncivilized patriarchal public world to practice the paid professions of the bar, the stock exchange. This woman seems to be practicing both kinds of professions at once. What has happened in these fifty-odd years to nullify Woolf's either/or analysis? And what is happening to the woman with the sick child? She seems to be having trouble keeping up with the men now that the procession has crossed the bridge.

Woolf did not tell us that the city of professions is built on a hillside. She did not say that the doors opening into law, medicine, politics, engineering, banking, and investment are situated on the heights and that the climb is steep. As the procession turns up the high road you can see some women still walking briskly, but others are stumbling, nay faltering. Surely their skirts are too narrow, their shoes too tight, their minds too occupied by home.

Woolf knew that for every person in the procession she watched, except perhaps those few women traipsing behind, there was someone at home practicing the unpaid professions. Today those "someones" have joined the procession. The daughters, sisters, wives, mothers of well-educated men, somewhat educated men, poorly educated men, uneducated men all walk across the bridge each morning into the paid professions or paid work of some kind. Whether by choice, circumstance, necessity, or some combination of the three, most walk back again into the unpaid ones.

But look now at those stragglers on the high road. Not the breathless women but the smiling, incongruously dressed ones who stop along the way to admire the view. They are actually passing the stumblers and together with their no-nonsense, gray-suited sisters are approaching the entrances when a woman nears! Still, give a strong push and the doors do open; indeed, women are going in and out as if they belong.

Does this mean that men's culture is being turned upside down, which is to say rightside up? Is politics becoming less competitive, the law less pugnacious, banking less acquisitive? Not to my knowledge. Yet some small changes are occurring. That woman in the flowing dress now entering the door marked medicine has just created a center for victims of violence at the city hospital. The research of the one in the full skirt who is just now opening the academy's portals is shaking the foundations of psychology. The biologist wearing overalls whose corn grows in the field over there is making her colleagues rethink both their theories and their methodologies. The actress walking through the stage door donates her earnings to peace organizations. That dancer is giving her money to a black women's college. That law professor is actively trying to change the legal system's understanding of pornography. That scientist is running her laboratory in an egalitarian manner. If Florence Nightingale "left the world better than she found it,"[24] if on our side of the deep sea Alice Hamilton, Jane Addams, Crystal Eastman, Helen Thompson Woolley did likewise, professional women today are also acting out Anna Petrovna's dream of turning at least their own small portions of the world upside down. Not all, probably not even a majority, possibly only a determined few. But at least that many.

Woolf might not call those women in the gray suits who are entering the doors of the professions contradictions, but by her own analysis those who would rather adapt than disturb are just that. Given still existing conceptions of masculinity and femininity, in acquiring the "manly" qualities of competitiveness, jealousy, pugnacity, and possessiveness yet being female human beings, these professionals are both women and not women. The contradictory nature of their position explains many of the problems they confront on the job and at home and is also reflected in such mundane matters as their decisions about dress; their uncertainty about whom to model their speech and behavior on in the university classroom, the courtroom, the board room, the operating room; and, of course, pronouncements such as the one by a Boston *Globe* music critic who said of the director of a renowned British ensemble touring American concert halls: "Brown is a first-rate violinist. And just like Olympic gold medalist Florence Griffith-Joyner, the strikingly lovely Brown is a woman who knows one can be both a champion in your field and triumphantly feminine. In the first half of the concert, she wore an elegant dark formal gown. In the second half for the concerto, she wore a springtime dress of dazzling white."[25]

Is it easier to fit into the professions than to be disturbing elements? Possibly, but the course Woolf would have us reject takes its toll. It is hard, very hard to be a living contradiction every minute and hour of every working day and night: The psychic costs are enormous and the threat of ridicule is ever present. Of course, for the women who refuse to or do not know how to fit in—the ones who remain relatively uncompetitive, unjealous, unpugnacious, and unacquisitive women— derision is not a threat but a fact of life. "Just an old bag who'd been hanging around Cold Spring Harbor for years" is what a famous biologist called Nobel scientist Barbara McClintock.[26] Most disturbing elements are schooled also in poverty and chastity.

But lest we take the burdens of being disturbances too much to heart, let us look again at the procession. What are those stumblers doing as our precious few try to disturb the existing constitution of things and their sisters attempt to adapt to it? Can they be walking back down the hill? Are they giving up and going home? No, few of them can afford to. They are joining that second, much bigger wave of women now spilling off the bridge and onto the low road, the one less traveled by men.

Woolf did not tell us that across the bridge two roads diverge. She did not say that fifty years later the choice for educated women, if "choice" is the right word for what so often is far from being voluntary, would be between walking up to the "male" professions on the heights or down to the "female" ones. See those doors marked teaching, nursing, social work? She did not say that women's options would consist of two kinds of paid professions, one high and the other low. Nor did she perhaps anticipate that the great majority would pick the "female" ones.

How astonishing that when women cross the bridge relatively few follow the men up the hill! Are the doors on the heights too heavy for the rest to open or have those women taking the road less traveled by men never wanted to be professors, directors, diplomats? Has the fear of being judged unnatural prevented them from ever imagining themselves heading a bank or embassy or did their self-confidence wane during their school and college years until they no longer trusted their own ability to survive as living contradictions? Perhaps the reason is simply that they see no way of combining the professions on the heights with the unpaid ones they want to practice. Or maybe these women truly want to help others.

Whatever the explanation of the unequal distribution of women in the two kinds of paid professions, Woolf would be interested to know that those entering the doors of the "female" professions, otherwise known as the "caring" professions, need take no special vows of poverty, chastity, and derision. These stern taskmistresses rule the lowlands. Wages here are perhaps enough to live on by oneself but they are not a penny more, not even for single mothers; you need not refuse to sell your brain for the sake of money for no money is ever offered you; as for fame and praise, they reside on the heights.

Will these educated women fulfill Anna Petrovna's dream of turning the world upside down? Working on both sides of the bridge in what amounts to a double shift, engaged in the unpaid and low-paid professions that they and their culture devalue, they are perhaps more likely to replicate her feelings of irrelevance and her sense of being a failure. Sharing her culture's valuation of the domestic activities she performed on her estate, Anna Petrovna did not count them as real work. Hence her frustration and unhappiness. Today, the professions that impose poverty, chastity, and derision on their practitioners comprise activities analogous to the ones performed at home by Chekhov's heroine. It is no accident that they are alternately called "the caring professions" and "women's professions." They involve the self-same activities and processes that our culture used to place in the private home and assign to women. Although they have been transported into the public world, they stand to the "male" occupations that Woolf was discussing in much the same relation as the domestic occupations Anna Petrovna performed on her estate stood to the ones of professor, director, diplomat she wished she had been allowed to undertake in the public world.

The Challenges for Educated Women

Standing on the bridge it is just possible to see a few women and men in the lowlands packing up their belongings. The cries of the people on the heights leave no doubt as to what is happening. "Join us up here you teachers, nurses, and social workers," they shout. "Not just for a visit. Come to stay. Forswear poverty, chastity, and derision forever. Come right now. We have ropes you can use to scale the rocks. Let us throw them down to you."

In response, more and more people are trying to drag their possessions lock, stock, and barrel up the face of the cliff. In view of our culture's devaluation of the caring professions, in view of the denigration that teachers, nurses, and social workers experience, who can blame them for trying to reach higher ground even by such an improbable route? Yet where prestige, fame, and money dwell can competition, jealousy, pugnacity, and possessiveness be far behind? I ask because so long as they are under the sway of three of Woolf's teachers, those who take the low road into the city of professions tend by default, if not by choice, to hold onto their senses. True, from the point of view of their professions these civilized teachers, nurses, social workers are not disturbing elements in Woolf's sense. How can they be when the "female" professions have not for the most part partaken of the war-related qualities possessed by the "male" professions Woolf had in mind? Nor do these women fulfill Anna Petrovna's ambition of turning the world upside down. Given the cultural devaluation of their occupations, they cannot. Many, however, succeed in the more modest ambition of making the world a better place by helping the young, the poor, the sick, the feeble, the elderly.

Listen now and you can hear some of these women warn the ones headed for the heights that upon reaching their destination this modest ambition may have to be forsworn. You can hear them protest that care cannot be nourished in a competitive environment; that the young, the poor, the sick, the feeble, the elderly cannot obtain the help they need where acquisitiveness and pugnaciousness prevail. If I am not mistaken these women are giving voice to Woolf's fear that with professionalization comes decivilization. In the past her anxiety may not have seemed to apply to the "caring" professions. Now, with the pressure mounting for their practitioners to become "genuine" professionals, the risk of losing one's senses also rises. But whereas Woolf's advice to the women walking off the bridge onto the high road matched Anna Petrovna's dream of turning the world upside down, it translates differently for the women whose professions are in transit. Were she still alive Woolf might well say: "You too must be disturbances for although your professions are not yet standing on their heads, they are listing dangerously. In your case, therefore, to disturb means both preventing your occupations from being turned upside down and pushing them back into the upright positions that they have long since abandoned."

But Woolf is not alive. She cannot see today's procession move across the bridge and into the city on the hillside and we cannot ask her if the poverty, chastity, and derision she prescribed are dangerous to women. We must ask ourselves, however, if those who have traditionally been cast in the role of self-sacrificer should really be expected to forego the personal rewards that "genuine" professions offer when after long and arduous struggles they finally manage to cross the bridge.

Woolf was keenly aware and sharply critical of the different wages paid men and women. She also knew full well the costs to women of the sacrifice of self that was so often the price of helping others. She did not say, but she might have—nay, she should have—that one challenge facing educated women who enter the "caring" professions is how to hold onto their senses, how to keep their fields and themselves civilized without being trapped in the stereotypical female role of self-sacrificer or even victim. She might have also said that another challenge is how to temper the care, concern, and connection that are absolutely essential to the sound practice of their professions with reason and critical analysis so that they do not lapse into a well-meaning but ineffectual sentimentality.

Woolf certainly knew that educated women at the heights face opposite problems. As she perceived so clearly, their first challenge is how to live in the realm of fame, money, prestige, and power without being corrupted. But an equally compelling one is how to temper the rationality, critical thinking, and self-governance that are the marks of a "genuine" professional with the care, concern, and connection that are absolutely essential to turning both the professions and the world around. Focusing on the manliness of the war-related qualities that govern "men's" professions, Woolf ignored what she knew to be the manliness of the reason, critical thinking, self-sufficiency, and self-governance that are supposed to characterize the educated people from whose ranks "genuine" professionals are drawn. Dwelling on what she took to be the evils for society of women becoming competitive, jealous, pugnacious, and possessive as soon as they crossed the bridge, she neglected the perils inherent in the separation of mind from body, thought from action, reason from feeling and emotion, and self from other that are built into our genderized definition of an educated person.[27]

Remarkably, those disturbing elements, those unsolemn women on the high road, those women who refuse to adapt somehow divest themselves of the "manly" forms of rationality and personal autonomy they learned in school—or did they manage never to "master" these in the first place? Holding onto their senses and their humanity as they practice their professions, they defy established codes by joining reason to passion and harnessing knowledge to the care, concern, and connection. If disturbances, they are also pioneers who on a daily basis are developing new ways to think and work in their chosen fields. Some women in the lowlands are pioneers too. Remaining free from an unreal loyalty to professionalization, they refuse to distance themselves from the interests and needs of their students, patients, clients. Making these interests and needs their own, they seek ways of linking impersonal knowledge to action and abstract theory to concrete practice.

But those few intrepid women at the heights and in the lowlands should not have to figure out, each for herself and every generation anew, how to bring together the qualities education and the professions tear asunder. It is too much to ask, too great a burden for them to bear, too difficult a task to undertake alone. I invited you to stand on the bridge with me to watch the procession. I see now that we must not linger here. There is too much work to be done in the city on the hillside.

The Challenges for Educators

Even as educated women face challenges themselves, they pose new ones for educators. First and foremost is how to make what each of Woolf's disturbing elements must now learn for herself—how to engage in a profession and remain civilized—part and parcel of the education of all so that succeeding generations of educated women will find it easier than ours has to fulfill Anna Petrovna's dream. Another is how to counteract the hidden curriculum of school and society that teaches all of us that the "caring" professions belong in the lowlands.

Far-reaching changes are required if the first challenge is to be met, for those pioneer women accomplish the impossible. Transforming themselves from living contradictions—females possessing the "manly" qualities—into people who transcend male as well as female stereotypes, they fuse qualities that some of our greatest philosophers have assured

us are incompatible and, as they are presently defined, certainly do
resist combination. Following Rousseau and Kant, we build disconnection
from others and from our own feelings and emotions into our very
concepts of rationality and autonomy and the suspension of critical
thought into our ideas of care, concern, and connection thus making it
impossible for a person to exhibit both sorts of qualities simultaneously.
Human "chameleons" and split personalities can prosper under this
scheme for it is possible to be rational at one moment and caring the
next. The pioneers in the city on the hillside do not, however, turn their
caring and their reason on and off. They exhibit both continuously.

With all the talk today about thinking, we need as researchers to
begin to think about these women. We need to make them our subjects
not in order to objectify them but to learn from their example how and
what to teach our young. As teachers and the teachers of teachers let
us not, however, sit back placidly to await the results of that research.
While the philosophers in our midst study these pioneers in order to
redefine and in the process degenderize rationality and autonomous
judgement—and care, concern, and connection; while the educational
theorists determine how, in light of these women's lives and work, to
do what Mill never dreamed of, namely reconstruct our culture's conception of an educated person; while experts in the various teaching
areas figure out how to map onto their respective subject matters the
"ansvars rationalitet" (the "caring rationality" or perhaps one should
call it the "responsive rationality")[28] our pioneer women exhibit; while
the curriculum specialists redesign the many programs focusing on
decisionmaking that now assume a sharp separation of the "manly"
and "womanly" qualities and honor only the former;[29] let us begin to
make those women who have been or now are disturbing elements in
Woolf's positive sense vivid presences in the school curriculum.

Quite apart from the fact that we do not yet fully understand how
these women accomplished what they did a century ago, or do it now,
incorporating their achievements into school curricula is a significant
challenge because the facts contradict the stereotypes that still prevail.
As a case in point, Florence Nightingale was not so much a Lady with
a Lamp as a woman who, reorganizing hospitals from top to bottom
in the Crimean War, performed the function of "an administrative
chief."[30] Once back in England she set out in an 800-page document
"vast principles of far reaching reform" that provided the basis for a
Royal Commission Report that for decades remained "the leading authority on the medical administration of armies."[31] Let us fill our
classrooms with Nightingale and her sisters, both historical and contemporary, real and fictional not in the capacity of role models or
exemplars but as examples of women who in their lives and work have

brought together and in the process transmuted the "manly" qualities of rationality, critical thinking, and autonomous action and the "womanly" ones of care, concern, connection, nurturance, and love.

Scholars who seek to transform the curriculum by integrating women into it call the introduction of exceptional women a first stage in a complex process and an elitist stage at that.[32] But our challenge is not to show the world that women have made their mark on history. It is to provide students with alternative modes of thinking, perceiving, acting, feeling, and existing in relation to others so that educated women can carry out Anna Petrovna's dream without having to reinvent for themselves the minutest details of daily life. When the examples are drawn from the entire population rather than a privileged segment of it—when they include black, Hispanic, and Asian as well as white women; old and young, married and single, mothers without partners and women without children—the project of giving Woolf's disturbing elements a central place in the curriculum takes on a new validity.

Of course, examples are not enough. Practice is also required. And of course, to meet the first challenge to educators our ideal of the educated person will have to be restructured. Because that ideal is linked tightly to the function our culture attributes to education of carrying out society's productive processes—by which I mean not just economic but political, social, and cultural ones as well—rather than its reproductive ones (and I define these broadly to include the rearing of children, caring for the sick, tending to the needs of family members) the fundamental premise upon which our whole educational system rests will also have to be rethought.[33] "Far-reaching changes" did I say? That is an understatement.

I spoke earlier of the importance of being sensitive to gender. Unless we take to heart the genderization of the attributes both included in and excluded from our present ideal, I do not think we can make the changes we must. Nor can we expect cultural attitudes toward the "caring" professions to change if we ignore the fact that they are also called "female."

In failing to acknowledge that the services provided by teaching, nursing, and social work constitute some of the central reproductive processes of society and that in our culture these have traditionally been considered women's responsibility, one remains blind to the value hierarchy that situates the "caring" professions in the lowlands and keeps them there. How many today would try to turn them into "genuine" professions without admitting that "genuine" means "male" and without ever quite saying that in the process care, concern, and connection will be replaced by the "virtues" of distance, objectivity, and efficiency! Be gender-*in*sensitive and, given the cultural value hierarchy that places

male above female and society's productive processes above its reproductive ones, one should not be surprised if in the course of that move
to the top of the hill the nurturant activity at the heart of each "caring"
profession is sacrificed.

The second educational challenge of how to keep the "caring"
professions *caring* without their practitioners having to sacrifice themselves in the manner of Anna Petrovna on her estate is not ours alone.
Yet as educators we can raise the offending value hierarchy to consciousness. We can try to counteract schooling's contribution to the
devaluation and denigration of women and of the positive functions
and traits that have been assigned us historically. We can think anew
about the significance of society's reproductive processes. As Woolf would
remind us, however, our goal is not to turn the value hierarchy upside
down. Our challenge is not how to move the "female" professions up
to the heights while banishing the "male" ones to the lowlands. It is
to find a middle ground where hierarchy vanishes: a large, open, inviting,
area midway up the hillside where the importance of society's reproductive
processes is recognized; where women, and men too, can practice the
"caring" professions without having to become uncivilized; and where
the professions now called "genuine" can be as caring as those whose
legitimacy is now denied.

Mill's program for educating women had two parts: that women be
given access to men's education and that society's practices and attitudes
be changed so that women who read and write, do history, philosophy,
and mathematics will not be viewed as contradictions. In *Three Guineas*
Woolf, for whom *The Subjection of Women* was required reading,[34] warned
against the first part. Beware men's education and the professions for
which it prepares them, she said. They lead to war. I am oversimplifying
what is perhaps an oversimplified analysis of the roots of war. Yet Woolf
is one of the few outspoken figures in our past who believed in women's
equality and also, for good reason, had qualms about men's education.
If she did not quite do justice to Mill's insight that women who cross
the bridge are already living contradictions, she more than compensated
for this shortfall by the attention she paid women as disturbing elements
in the existing constitution of things. Prescribing a regimen of resistance
and reform, she cast women as agents of change in a culture attached
to war. Making women's capacity to be disturbances a virtue possessing
moral, political, and social significance and demanding that women act
it out on a public stage, she implied that the way to overcome women's
contradictory status is for each in her own way to turn Anna Petrovna's
dream into a reality.

How can the young of this country be civilized human beings,
people who oppose both war and the destruction of the environment,

if their teachers are not? Educated women whose concern is gender and education are in the enviable position of not only being disturbances but of helping to form new generations of educated women who will walk across the bridge determined to make the world a better place to live. For all this, John Stuart Mill thanks you, Virginia Woolf thanks you, Anna Petrovna thanks you, and I thank you.

Notes

1. John Stuart Mill, *The Subjection of Women* (Cambridge: M.I.T. Press, 1970), 29. Wendell Robert Carr in his introduction to this edition (p. vi) gives this date. Publication was not until 1869.

2. Ibid., xxi.

3. "Women Account for Half of College Enrollment in U.S., 3 other Nations," *Chronicle of Higher Education*, September 17, 1986.

4. Virginia Woolf, *Three Guineas* (New York: Harcourt Brace Jovanovich, 1938), 72. References to this work will henceforth appear in parentheses in the text.

5. Immanuel Kant, "Of the Distinction of the Beautiful and Sublime in the Interrelations of the Two Sexes" in *Philosophy of Woman*, ed. Mary Briody Mahowald (Indianapolis: Hackett Publishing, 1983), 194.

6. Ibid., 194–195.

7. Arnold Schopenhauer, "On Women," in *Philosophy of Women*, ed. Mahowald, 229.

8. Jean-Jacques Rousseau, *Emile*, trans. Allan Bloom (New York: Basic Books, 1979), 409.

9. Ibid., 364.

10. Mills, *The Subjection of Women*, 22.

11. In using the word "appropriating," I definitely do *not* mean to imply that women did not actively work and struggle to obtain this education.

12. The material from here to the end of the next section follows closely Jane Roland Martin, "The Contradiction of the Educated Woman," *Forum for Honors*, 18(1987):6–12.

13. "Women Account for Half of College Enrollment in U.S., 3 Other Nations," *Chronicle of Higher Education*, Sept. 17, 1986.

14. Roberta M. Hall and Bernice Sandler, "The Classroom Climate: A Chilly One for Women?" (Washington, D.C.: Project on the Status and Education of Women, 1982); Roberta M. Hall and Bernice Sandler, "Out of the Classroom: A Chilly Campus Climate for Women?" (Washington, D.C.: Project on the Status and Education of Women, 1984). Dale Spender, *Invisible Women* (London: Writers and Readers Publishing Cooperative Society, 1982).

15. Spender, *Invisible Women*.

16. For a discussion of Plato as the source of this hypothesis, see Jane Roland Martin, *Reclaiming a Conversation* (New Haven: Yale University Press, 1985), Ch. 2.

17. Alexandra G. Kaplan and Mary Anne Sedney, *Psychology and Sex Roles: An Androgynous Perspective* (Boston: Little, Brown & Co., 1980); Rosemary Deem, *Women and Schooling* (London: Routledge & Kegan Paul, 1978); Nancy Frazier and Myra Sadker, *Sexism in School and Society* (New York: Harper & Row, 1972); Ann Oakley, *Sex, Gender and Society* (New York: Harper & Row, 1972).

18. Elizabeth Beardsley, "Traits and Genderization" in *Feminism and Philosophy*, ed. Mary Vetterling-Braggin, Frederick A. Elliston, and Jane English (Totowa, N.J.: Littlefield, Adams, 1977), 117–123. Beardsley used the term *genderization* to refer to language. I use it to refer to the traits themselves.

19. See, e.g., I. K. Broverman, S. R. Vogel, D. M. Broverman, F. E. Rosenkrantz and P. S. Rosenkrantz, "Sex Role Stereotypes: A Current Appraisal," *Journal of Social Issues*, 38(1972):59–78.

20. For further development of this idea see Martin, *Reclaiming a Conversation*, Ch. 7.

21. Alex Zwerdling, *Virginia Woolf and the Real World* (Berkeley: University of California Press, 1986), 240.

22. Patricia Jagentowicz Mills, "Hegel and 'The Woman Question': Recognition and Intersubjectivity" in *The Sexism of Social and Political Theory*, ed. Lorenne M.G. Clark and Lynda Lange (Toronto: University of Toronto Press, 1979), 94.

23. Anton Chekhov, *Wild Honey*, trans. and adapted by Michael Frayn (London: Methuen, 1984), 95.

24. Carolyn Heilbrun, *Toward a Recognition of Androgyny* (New York: Alfred A. Knopf, 1973), 138.

25. Anthony Tommasini, Boston *Globe*, October 8, 1988, 16.

26. Evelyn Fox Keller, *A Feeling for the Organism* (San Francisco: W. H. Freeman, 1983), 141.

27. For further discussion of these separations, see Martin, *Reclaiming a Conversation*, especially Ch. 7.

28. I borrow this Danish phrase from Kirsten Reisby who in turn credits Hildur Ve. According to Reisby, "ansvars" can be translated in English as either "caring" or "responsibility." She prefers "responsibility" and I am taking the liberty here of going one step further and interpreting responsibility as responsiveness.

29. For a discussion of programs in moral education having this focus, see Jane Roland Martin, "Transforming Moral Education," *The Journal of Moral Education*, 16(1987):204–213.

30. Lytton Strachey, *Eminent Victorians* (London: Chatto & Windus, 1918), 135; cf. Heilbrun, *Toward a Recognition of Androgyny*, 138–142.

31. Heilbrun, *Toward a Recognition of Androgyny*, 157.

32. Peggy McIntosh, "Interactive Phases of Curricular Re-vision: A Feminist Perspective," Working Paper 124, Wellesley College, Center for Research on Women, 1983; cf. Marilyn R. Schuster and Susan R. Van Dyne, "Stages of Curriculum Transformation" in *Women's Place in the Academy* (Totowa, N.J.: Roman & Allanheld, 1985).

33. For a fuller discussion of this point see Martin, *Reclaiming a Conversation*.

34. Zwerdling, *Virginia Woolf and the Real World*, 211–212.

ABOUT THE BOOK AND EDITORS

Recent feminist research has demonstrated how women have been neglected or misrepresented in virtually every discipline in the humanities and social sciences. The most exciting research growing out of this body of work is the attempt to see what kinds of changes are required in the assumptions, results, and even the methods of these disciplines to give women's perspectives and values full credit.

In this important volume, we have a progress report in which some of the most active scholars in the feminist movement survey the results of feminist research in their respective fields. They examine the inherent biases that are being overcome and the new perspectives that are emerging in what has become a virtual revolution in the social sciences and humanities.

Revolutions in Knowledge is an indispensable book not only for feminist scholars and their students but for anyone who cares about how scholarship is conducted and about what is happening at its frontiers.

Sue Rosenberg Zalk is director of the Center for the Study of Women and Society at the Graduate School of the City University of New York and professor of psychology in the Department of Educational Foundations and Counseling Programs at Hunter College. She is coauthor of *Women's Realities, Women's Choices* and *Expectant Fathers* and is the editor for *Sex Roles: A Journal of Research.* **Janice Gordon-Kelter** is grants assistant in the development office at the University of St. Thomas–Houston and former assistant director of the Center for the Study of Women and Society at the Graduate School of the City University of New York. She has a Ph.D. in history and is the author of numerous articles on medieval history.

ABOUT THE CONTRIBUTORS

Rebecca M. Blank is associate professor at Northwestern University with joint appointments in the Department of Economics, the School of Education and Social Policy, and the Center for Urban Affairs and Public Policy. Her research interests focus on the interactions between the labor market, public policy, and the behavior and well-being of the low-income population.

Susan A. Farrell is a graduate student in sociology and women's studies at the Graduate School, the City University of New York. She was managing editor of *Gender and Society* from 1987–1990 and coeditor of *The Social Construction of Gender* (with Judith Lorber, 1991).

Cheryl Townsend Gilkes is John D. and Catherine T. MacArthur Associate Professor of Sociology and African American Studies at Colby College. Her articles have appeared in the *Journal of Religious Thought, Journal of Feminist Studies in Religion, Signs,* and *Psychology of Women Quarterly.*

Virginia Held is professor of philosophy at Hunter College and the Graduate School, the City University of New York. Her most recent book is *Rights and Goods: Justifying Social Action.* She is on the editorial boards of *Ethics, Hypatia, Political Theory, Public Affairs Quarterly,* and *Social Theory and Practice.*

Dorothy O. Helly is professor of history and women's studies at Hunter College, the City University of New York. Her publications include the Hunter College Women's Studies Collective, *Women's Realities, Women's Choices* (1983); *Livingstone's Legacy: Horace Waller and Victorian Mythmaking* (1987); and *Connected Domains: Beyond the Public/Private Dichotomy (Essays from the Seventh Berkshire Conference on the History of Women)* (edited with Susan Reverby, forthcoming).

Jane Roland Martin, professor of philosophy at the University of Massachusetts–Boston, is author of *Reclaiming a Conversation: The Ideal of the Educated Woman* and of numerous articles on gender and education and gender and science.

Mary Brown Parlee is professor of psychology at the Graduate School, the City University of New York. She is the author of numerous professional articles and chapters on the psychology of menstruation and premenstrual syndrome and also writes about psychology for the general public. She is past president of the Division of the Psychology of Women of the American Psychological Association.

Rayna Rapp is professor of anthropology at the New School for Social Research and is currently completing a book on the social impacts and cultural meaning of prenatal diagnosis. She is editor of *Toward an Anthropology of Women* and has published on gender and kinship; class and family relations; and the new reproductive technologies in both popular and scholarly journals.

Joan C. Tronto is associate professor of political science and women's studies at Hunter College, the City University of New York. Her research interests include women and U.S. politics and the ethic of care. She is at work on a book entitled *Moral Boundaries*, about feminist politics and morality.